JUMP

To Ancestor Stories in Space and Time

Laurie Labak

Copyright © 2025 Laurie Labak

All rights reserved

Cover design by the author.

No part of this book may be reproduced, or stored in a retrieval system, or transmitted in any form or by any means, electronic, mechanical, photocopying, recording, or otherwise, without express written permission of the publisher.

ISBN - 9798262838363

Library of Congress Control Number: 2018675309
Printed in the United States of America

CONTENTS

Title Page
Copyright
Chapter 1 Connect   2
Chapter 2 Adam   3
Chapter 3 New World   20
Chapter 4   Westward   36
Chapter 5 John and Caroline   50
Chapter 6 Prairieland   59
Chapter 7 First Responder   64
Chapter 8 D - Day   73
Chapter 9 Chicagoland   93
Chapter 10 Landing Place   98

Jump

to ancestor stories in space and time

by

Laurie Labak

CHAPTER 1 CONNECT

I invite you to J-U-M-P with me on a trampoline of space and time. Ancestors are waiting to share their stories with you.

Where will we land? An immigrant ship, a bloody battlefield. An Indian camp, a prisoner-of-war camp. A Dakota farm, a Chicago bungalow. A Scottish castle, a Colorado ranch. The stories are not fiction or fable. Not myth or fantasy. The stories describe real events and real people.

These ancestor stories emerged from historic records, old newspapers, oral histories, family genealogies and websites. The stories recorded here are as short or as long as needed for the telling. No artificial intelligence AI was used in the editing and retelling.

Are you ready to step with me on our trampoline of space and time? Take a breath. Bend your knees.

J – U – M – P !

CHAPTER 2   ADAM

B-17

Our first J-U-M-P in space and time takes us into the skies of wartime Europe. The year is 1944. Our B-17 bomber plane is on fire. We enter the true story of Adam Klosowski, son of Polish immigrants and family cousin of my husband Alex Labak. This is Adam's story from his interviews with a Minnesota newspaper reporter in 1995.

Photo from Adam Klosowski family

Adam Klosowski enlisted in the Army Air Corps in 1942 after Japan bombed Pearl Harbor. After training in aircraft mechanics and gunnery, Adam was assigned to a B-17 bomber plane. Each B-17 flew with a crew of ten. Pilot, co-pilot, navigator, engineer, radio man, bombardier and four gunners.

Adam was a waist gunner positioned in the middle of the plane and armed with a mounted 50 - caliber machine gun. The plane was known as the Flying Fortress. Adam said, "The B-17 was designed to withstand a lot of damage and still fly."

Adam's Eighth Air Force became the largest military unit in World War II. Adam was stationed at one of eighty American military bases in England.

Before every bombing mission came a briefing. Then each crew assembled their flight gear and boarded a truck to the airfield and their B-17. The crew of ten checked their tanks of fuel, oil, and oxygen. Adam said, "We made sure the ground crew hadn't goofed up." Then they waited for orders.

Pilots never started their engines until ready for take-off. Then thirty bombers, each with four engines of 1350 horsepower, all started up at once. The ground beneath the air base rumbled with the sound. The bombers took off at ninety-second intervals.

Once in the air, each pilot looked for a plane firing red or green or yellow flares. Planes would move toward their assigned color and form up as a group. The pilot knew his position in that group. They would gain altitude and head for the continent and the city or target they were assigned.

Adam said, "It was a major operation to get all those planes up." There were times when the air base command officers ordered over a thousand planes up in one day. Ground crews at the air bases were responsible for maintaining and supplying all those planes.

In World War II the Army Air Corps lost nearly eight thousand bomber planes to enemy fire. Adam said, "Clearly the most dangerous place to be in the air was in a bomber over Germany."

Daily losses were so high that the Allies considered giving up daytime bombing raids. There were 26,000 men killed in action and 18,000 men wounded in action. Twenty-eight thousand men were taken prisoners-of- war, and 78,000 men were missing in action.

Skies Over Germany

In 1944 the B-17 bomber planes were at the mercy of powerful German anti-aircraft guns. Losses were heavy. Adam said, "One time the air base sent out 25 planes and none came back."

On Adam's first bombing run his plane jerked and shuddered as 105 - millimeter shells exploded below them. On every mission Adam was afraid his plane would get a direct hit and burst into flames.

B-17 and flak from enemy fire

World War II military photo archives

Adam and the other gunners swiveled their machine guns to take aim and fire on the fast and deadly Luftwaffe fighter planes. The four gunners endured the roar of engines and exploding flak bursts. Air turbulence shook and rocked the plane.

"We were flying over France when we came in at 12,000 feet for a bombing run." Through patchy clouds the crew could see other bomber formations scattered across the skies. One planeload of bombs hit an ammunition dump. "The explosions created a wall of flames half a mile high."

One time Adam's crew was flying over Germany, dropping bombs on fuel plants and refineries. German fighter planes attacked the B-17 bomber formation ahead of Adam's plane. "I saw falling engines and wreckage, then parachutes with men, all going down."

On Adam's B-17 every gunner was firing, including Adam. In the 9 o'clock position Adam saw a fighter plane he'd never seen before. "What in the hell is that?" When the strange plane came into view below their plane, the ball turret gunner shot it up.

Adam watched the plane spin and crash. The crew learned later it was a new type of German fighter jet with a speed of 650 miles an hour. The Allies' best propeller planes had a top speed of 450 miles an hour. "The Germans had an advantage," said Adam, "but they got their jet fighters too late to turn around the war."

One morning Adam's B-17 crew flew off into a clear blue sky. Adam said, "It looked like every plane in England was in flight." That morning the briefing officer had told them, "I don't want even one plane coming back with bombs in their belly. Drop them on anything that looks worthwhile." Their mission targets had already been hit, so Adam's group of B-17s turned to go home.

Adam's crew flew over some military barracks. The bombardier said, "This looks as good as anything. We'll take this." Later, back at the air base, the crew learned that the barracks they bombed were not housing German soldiers. The barracks were sheltering refugees from bombed-out cities. Adam said, "We blew the place to nothing and killed a whole lot of German civilians that time."

Hard Landing

In October 1944 Adam was flying his seventeenth mission. Their target was a German aircraft assembly plant. After the bombs dropped Adam thought, "Boy we've got it made. We're going home." But then anti-aircraft shells started coming up and closing in on either side. "Now I just knew we were going to get it."

Another burst of shells came up. Adam saw gasoline pouring out of the wing behind the B17's number three engine. "It scared the daylights out of me." Adam radioed the pilot to cut the number three engine, which the pilot did immediately.

The ball turret gunner crawled out with glass embedded in his bloody face. The co-pilot's oxygen line was shot off. The pilot hooked him up to an emergency bottle of oxygen.

Now all four engines were dead because all the gas lines were shot up. The pilot switched on the "BAIL OUT" alarm. When the bombardier bailed out, his parachute harness caught on the door frame. He had to pull himself back in and free his harness strap before he could bail out again.

Adam was the last man to jump from the plane. "My chute opened. What a beautiful sight." From his parachute at 2500 feet Adam watched his plane go down in a slow, wide spiral. It slammed into a farmhouse in one huge ball of fire and smoke.

Captured

Adam landed in a plowed field. The hard landing sprained both his ankles. He could not run or even walk. "I just gave up and lay there." Some civilians came. "They had a heated argument in German whether or not to beat me up." An old uniformed soldier, part of the German home guard, rode up on a bicycle. He carried a battered rifle with a long bayonet. Adam thought, "This is no good at all."

The old soldier calmed down the civilians and did not harm Adam. A boy came pushing a wheelbarrow. Soon Adam was sitting in the wheelbarrow on top of his parachute while the boy pushed the wheelbarrow down the trail toward the nearby village. All the people came behind, excited and chattering. The old German soldier followed on his bicycle. "We were quite a sight," said Adam.

In the village a civilian policeman pulled up on his motorcycle and took Adam to the police station. To Adam's surprise the men at the police station did not harm him. One man told him, "You go to prison camp, you play feetsball." The policeman did not know what German prison camps were like.

The men took Adam to a telephone operator's office so they could phone the nearby German military camp. An old man was at the telephone switchboard. The man said to Adam, "America g-u-u-t. Mine brother Ooo-ee-ooh." He might have meant Ohio.

A few hours later a military truck pulled up. Two German soldiers searched Adam and took one of his military ID dog tags. Adam still couldn't walk, so the soldiers half-carried him and boosted him into the back of the truck.

Two of Adam's B-17 crew buddies, the navigator and the co-pilot, were in the truck, along with a wooden coffin. The men knew the body in the coffin wasn't one of their crew because they all had survived the bail out.

The truck drove on, picking up more captured airmen. One was a badly burned P-47 fighter pilot. Another was the radio man from Adam's crew. The radio man was in severe pain with a broken leg and a broken arm. Adam said, "After he landed some kids beat the daylights out of him. He was in real sad shape."

One time when the truck was stopped a young German boy came alongside the truck. The boy asked Adam in perfect English, "When will the war be over?" Adam looked at him and said, "For me the war is over. For you I don't know when it will be over."

The Guard

The truck carrying the captured airmen arrived in Bremen, Germany just after an Allied bombing raid on the city. One of their guards, an older man, stayed with the captives on a street corner while the other guard went to find the Bremen railroad station.

While they waited, a young German soldier came by. When the soldier saw the captured American air crew he began to scream and yell at them. Soon a dozen angry men gathered around. "I knew what was going on," Adam said. The B-17 navigator could understand German. Adam saw the navigator's face turn the color of old newspaper.

The guard and the angry young soldier got into a shouting match. The guard took out his revolver, pulled the hammer back and pointed it at the German soldier. The guard said, "Eins, zwei, drei, vier. Laufes mit, du schwein." Walk away, you pig. The young soldier and all the men backed away and left.

Adam figured their guard had been ordered to deliver the air crew to the German interrogation center and that's what he was determined to do. Adam said, "I owe my life to that guard. The mob was going to have a necktie party."

Interrogation

The captives were loaded onto a train to Frankfurt. They traveled for three days and nights with no food and no water. Allied bombing raids had reduced the city of Frankfurt to ruins. The streets were narrow pathways cleared of rubble.

"When civilians saw us, they went absolutely wild. They screamed and yelled and threw stuff at us." The men were taken onto another train to the interrogation center. Again they got nothing to eat and they were very weak.

Most of Adam's B-17 air crew were together on the train. Adam and the tail gunner both had sprained ankles. The co-pilot had been on his first mission when their plane was shot down. He was still in a state of shock and never spoke to the others.

The navigator and Adam had been carrying the radio man with the broken leg and broken arm. But at the interrogation center they were too weak to carry him. Two Russian prisoners were ordered to carry the injured radio man away. Adam and the crew did not see the radio man again.

At the interrogation center the guards pushed Adam into a six foot by six foot cell. "I was just so tired I didn't care where I was at." After three days in solitary confinement Adam was taken for his interrogation. He gave the German officer his name, rank, and serial number.

The officer looked at some papers and said, "You are in the 486 bomb group, in the 833 squadron." Adam said, "You know more about me than I do." The German officer said, "That's all, get out of here." And that was the extent of Adam's interrogation.

Prison Camp

All the prisoners at the interrogation center were separated into groups. Adam and the American air crews were sent by train to Stalag Luft IV, a German prisoner-of-war camp in Poland. Then they were force marched two miles to the prison camp. Adam walked with two sprained ankles. He was weak and starving.

Stalag Luft IV was huge, with 2500 men in each of four sections. There were ten thousand prisoners in all. Adam was issued a spoon and a blanket. His group of thirty men was assigned to a room that was 16 feet by 32 feet.

There wasn't room for all the men to sleep on the floor. Adam slept on a table and used his shoes for a pillow. The barrack buildings were each about 120 feet long with rooms, hallway and a single toilet. All the windows were broken out. Winter was coming.

Adam's B-17 air crew had a new mission. They must try to stay alive until the war was over. Sometimes the prisoners got news about the war. It was a sad day when they learned about the Battle of the Bulge.

Some of the prisoners had been in the camp more than two years and were in bad shape. Adam said, "I thought I would die in that place. We weren't badly beaten or tortured. We just didn't get any food."

The main camp rations were soybeans that were full of worms. Adam ate the cooked worms along with the cooked soybeans. "There's protein in a worm." Prisoners ate out of tin cans that were never washed. Sometimes they got a small boiled potato or a piece of bread and margarine.

One time the prison camp received some musical instruments sent from an American YMCA. A man in the next barrack was from Louisiana. "He really could play a saxophone," said Adam.

All the prisoners liked the New Orleans-style music on the saxophone. Then Stalag Luft headquarters ordered, "No music after dark." The outside guards had been listening to the American jazz music instead of patrolling the prison grounds.

Christmas is a sacred holiday in Germany. The prison guards let the men go outside Christmas Eve, a beautiful starlit night. The prisoners walked around and sang holiday carols. On Christmas Day they each got an entire Red Cross parcel instead of the usual one-quarter parcel a week. "Those Red Cross parcels kept us alive," said Adam.

Sometime after Christmas the air crew's radio man was brought into prison camp. He had been treated for his broken leg and broken arm in a German civilian hospital. The radio man was shocked to see his old air crew and to see conditions in the prison camp. "He didn't think human beings could live like that."

One of the German guards was a big man about six feet six. "He had big hands and a mouth to match," Adam said. Even the other German guards were afraid of him. He liked to hit a prisoner across the side of the head with his open hand and break the prisoner's eardrum.

Many years later at a prisoner-of-war reunion Adam heard some guys talking. They said that after the camp was liberated someone found the body of the big German guard, but without his head. "Somebody got to him."

One time some German SS troops brought about 150 civilians into the camp. The group stayed in the camp overnight and the next morning they were marched away. Adam saw the SS men beat the civilian prisoners with rifle butts and prod them with bayonets. "They were a sad looking bunch." Adam never found out where they came from or where they were being taken.

Forced March

Now it was February 1945. The Russian troops were advancing and the prisoners could hear artillery fire. Prison camp commanders started moving the 10,000 men out.

The sick and wounded were moved by train. The rest of the prisoners were split up into groups of 500. For days Adam and all the men were force marched in long columns five men across. They spent each night in farmyard barns.

Some guards would scout ahead and try to get some potatoes if the farmer was cooperative. One time the guards brought out a big kettle of boiled barley. When the starving men in back began to push, the men in front panicked and the kettle was knocked to the ground. Some men scooped up the barley, dirt and all, but most of the men got nothing.

Adam was cold, exhausted, and weak from lack of food. Hundreds of German civilians of all ages were also walking along the road. Some rode in horse-drawn farm wagons. There was nothing for the horses to eat. The hungry prisoners would see dead horses along the road. They wanted some of that horse meat, but the guards wouldn't stop the march.

The next part of their evacuation was by train. They were packed into boxcars upright with standing room only. "We traveled on those boxcars for two days with no food to another prison camp." By then Adam was very weak from starvation. "We walked into that prison camp in real bad shape."

Some English prisoners saw Adam's crew and said to the guards, "Give our food to those Americans. We'll go without." The prisoners could hear distant artillery fire as the Russians advanced. They were given very little food.

Hitler's Jewish Solution

After several days Adam and the American prisoners were marched out with a different group of guards. "A bunch of old men," Adam said. The guards were men from Poland. After the German occupation of Poland some of the Polish men were given three options. Be a slave farm laborer or a German prison guard or go to a concentration camp.

Adam spoke in Polish with one of the guards. The guard said earlier in the war he was ordered to a work detail. German troops took all the Jews of his Polish village to a patch of woods and shot them every one. "The old Polish guard was still very upset about the killings he witnessed," Adam said.

One night the prisoners stayed in a barn that had a stack of wheat bundles. Nearby was a pile of bags filled with ashes to be used for fertilizer. Adam said, "It didn't smell too good in that shed."

Adam learned the farm was near the Nazi death camp at Bergen-Belsen in northern Germany. The farmer had ordered slave laborers from the Bergen-Belsen concentration camp to spread crematory ashes for fertilizer on his farmland.

Escape

In early April 1945 Adam heard rumors that Hitler had ordered the execution of all American airmen prisoners. Adam and his friend Grant, the B-17 ball turret gunner, made a plan. They would leave the forced march and make their way west to the Allied front.

Adam and Grant escaped the next night by crawling past the

guards. The two escaped prisoners were on the move behind enemy lines for the next thirteen days. They walked in the dark of night. They hid and rested during daylight hours. They lived on seed potatoes, pea vines and rhubarb they stole at night from farm fields and gardens.

"What tension," said Adam. "We never knew what would be ahead." One night Adam and Grant walked into a practice range for a German artillery battery. Another night Adam walked around a pine tree and saw a German soldier putting on his back pack. Adam stepped behind another tree and they got away.

They waded chest deep through icy ditch water to a spruce stand where they hid and dried out. One night they walked the rails on a railroad grade. Near daylight they came to a grassy swamp. They found a little island just big enough to hide and sleep for the day.

Another morning Adam and Grant saw German military barracks with people walking around. They crawled under the low branches of a tall spruce tree to hide for the day. In the afternoon a man came by with an axe and a little dog. The man chopped down a small tree close to where Adam and Grant were hiding.

The man's little dog began to run around and around their hiding place, yapping away. "Oh boy," Adam thought, "he's going to check what his dog found. We've had it." But the man picked up his little tree, walked away and never looked back to see what the dog was barking at.

Hunger

One time the men hid and rested in a large culvert under a German autobahn. All day they heard the rumbling of heavy military equipment passing over the culvert. Another night with the light of a full moon they dug out new seed potatoes with their hands. In a nearby pine grove they made a little fire and ate all the potatoes.

Later in the day the farmer came out. "He wasn't a bit happy to find his potato patch scratched up." Another time Adam found a farmer's feed bin and stole some ground oats meant for the farmer's dairy cows. Adam picked out the oat hulls and used a coffee can to cook the grain with water. Grant said to Adam, "The best cereal I ever had."

Adam and Grant walked through a night of cold rain, then hid and rested all the next day in cold rain. After dark they started walking again. They passed some parked German military vehicles. "I was pretty nervous then."

They came to stone farm buildings clustered together as in medieval times. They found a shed with straw on the second floor. A good place to dry out and rest. They climbed to the loft and kicked a hole in scruffy straw bales to make a nest and sleep.

A man's voice woke them up, "Das ist geneg." That is enough. Adam and Grant heard some men walk out of the shed, slam the door and leave. The men were German soldiers and they had pulled out several rows of straw bales while the tired escapees slept. If the soldiers had moved the next tier of bales, Adam and Grant would have fallen on top of their heads.

That night the two men were desperately hungry. They came to a long low building full of brood sows. In one of the pens were two calves. They took one of the calves out the door and down the trail.

"We hit the calf over the head with a rock and killed it. We ripped it open, cooked the liver in our coffee can and ate the whole thing." They cut off more meat, cooked it and threw it in a bag. They knew the farmer was going to search for his missing calf.

Shots Fired

One night in a pine forest Adam and Grant found cases of German rifle ammunition. "I knew we were not in a good place." They ran toward a couple of juniper trees.

By now they both had good night vision. They saw lumps that might be sentries. As they ran they heard two machine guns shooting. "Tracer bullets went by and we dropped down in the grass."

The men shooting at them were only about 150 feet away. Adam told Grant, "Let's take our chances and surrender." They shouted, "We give up." One of the soldiers said, "Get up." Adam and Grant realized they had surrendered to British soldiers, not German soldiers. They had reached the Allied line.

Rescue

The British infantrymen brought Adam and Grant a pail of warm water and soap. Adam said, "We must have been a sight. We were starving, ragged, dirty, stinking, and covered with lice." They were taken to a field kitchen and given a breakfast. Eggs, bacon, toast, oatmeal and a cup of tea. Adam said, "I ate it all. I craved that nourishment."

Adam and Grant were taken to a reception center set up by the Allies. The camp held several thousand displaced people from Eastern Europe. The British soldiers did not understand Slavic languages. "I got the job of translating English to Polish," said Adam.

Adam and Grant were taken to England to an American army hospital. "What a beautiful sight, with green grass growing all around and an American flag flying."

Adam was in bad shape after eight months as a prisoner of war. Adam weighed 110 pounds. Grant weighed 95 pounds. They were hospitalized for three weeks for malnutrition.

Adam suffered mentally from the stress of prison camp and their harrowing escape. "I stopped talking," said Adam. "I only spoke if I had to." Grant was able to send a telegram to his parents, but Adam could not put together the words for a telegram or letter to his family back home. "I just didn't care about anything," said Adam. "I ate and slept."

Home To Irene

One day news came to the hospital over the British radio, "The war is over. London is wild!"

Adam arrived home to his family in late June 1945. Adam's fiancée Irene had waited four years for his return. They married that fall. Adam and Irene Klosowski raised a family and managed a dairy herd on their farm in northern Minnesota. They shared a long and beautiful life together.

In 1996 Irene Klosowski sent me Adam's story from their local newspaper along with a hand-written letter. Irene wrote, "He never forgot. Lots of people don't believe it was so bad. (I) hope the young people now days never have to go thru that, and appreciate the good country and living we have."

In his interviews Adam said he often thought about the human cost of the war. His Eighth Air Force lost 94,000 personnel. After the war Adam and Irene met with other prison camp survivors at reunion conventions. Adam shared a lifelong bond with them.

"Freedom is not cheap. We should keep a very effective military force." Adam said, "You don't know how dear freedom is until you lose it. We almost lost it in World War II."

CHAPTER 3   NEW WORLD

Family Ties

My ancestor John Kingsley sailed from England to America in the year 1635. He brought with him the Puritan values of honest work and Christian duty. His story is recorded in the book Kingsley Family of America compiled by William Kingsley in 1980. Listed below is the paternal Kingsley lineage from father to son.

John Kingsley 1605-1678 arrived in America in 1635 and had five children.

John's son Eldad Kingsley 1638-1679 had six children.

Eldad's son, another John Kingsley 1665-1733 had twelve children.

John's son Ezra 1698-1759 had eight children.

Ezra's son Salmon 1723- 1813 had twelve children.

Salmon's son Ebenezer 1747-1800 had seven children.

Ebenezer's son, also named Ebenezer 1774 -1858 had fifteen children.

Ebenezer's son Edward W 1818-1883 had fifteen children.

Edward W's son Edward E 1855-1934 had twelve children.

The Kingsleys in America faithfully followed the biblical edict to be fruitful and multiply. Some families raised twelve to fifteen children. There were many hundreds of descendants.

Edward E Kingsley 1855-1934 was my great grandfather.

In 2009 another descendant, Ronald A Kingsley, compiled a family history of Edward E and Christina Kingsley. Ronald Kingsley, his wife Faye and his daughter Becky documented four generations of descendants of Edward E and Christina Kingsley.

Now we return to John Kingsley's descendants, but this time we will bring daughters into the family lineup. One of Edward E Kingsley's seven daughters was Caroline Kingsley Murray 1895 - 1985 who raised seven children.

Caroline's son Roy Murray 1917 – 1998 had five children. Roy Murray was my father.

I am Loretta (Laurie) Murray born 1947. I married Alex Labak in 1967.

Our four children and four grandchildren await a family historian of a future generation.

John And Elizabeth

I invite you to J-U-M-P again on the trampoline of space and time. We will travel to the early days of colonial settlement in America. John Kingsley, an Englishman and a Puritan, arrived at Massachusetts Bay in 1635 with his wife and daughter.

John and Elizabeth left England during a time of civil unrest and religious persecution. The young couple named their baby daughter Freedom. What did "Freedom" mean to John and Elizabeth Kingsley as they started their life together in the New World?

John and Elizabeth raised their five children in the settlement of Rehoboth in Plymouth Colony. John Kingsley was farmer, landowner and church founder.

A Kingsley story goes like this. When John was an old man in poor health, the town of Rehoboth was at war with the Wampamoag tribe. The tribal chief, known as King Philip, wanted to stop English settlement on his lands. Dozens of settlements were destroyed or damaged.

Rehoboth was attacked in 1676. Forty houses burned. John Kingsley's house and barn were set fire and burned along with all his livestock. The Kingsley family escaped to a fortified garrison house in the town.

Food was running out. John Kingsley wrote a letter to his preacher friend in Hartford, Connecticut. The spelling is his own. "It is betur to die by sord then famen ... I beg in my Lordes name to send us some meal."

John's preacher friend in Hartford persuaded the Connecticut War Council to send provisions to the starving refugees in Rehoboth. The Indian war ended when Chief Philip was killed August 1676.

John Kingsley died two years later. John's will revealed his close bond with his son Eldad. The will also revealed John's profound disdain for his son-in-law, John French, husband of John Kingsley's oldest daughter named Freedom.

John declared in his will, "I look that Eldad and his (children) to be a staffe to us in our old age, for John French hath left me in my old age when I had most need of him."

John Kingsley's gravestone of 1678

photos from William A Kingsley, 1980

John Kingsley's gravestone was lost, then rediscovered in 1890.

In 1664 John Kingsley's son Eldad built a house for his family in Rehoboth, Massachusetts Colony. The two story colonial-style house that Eldad built still stands, now more than three hundred years old.

house built by Eldad Kingsley 1664

photo from William A Kingsley, 1980

The King's Lea

Where did the name Kingsley come from? We know a village named Kingsley is near the English seaport of Bournemouth, where John Kingsley set sail for America in 1635.

The name Kingsley first appeared in the year 1086 in The Domesday Book, a list of all the lands and land owners of Britain.

The Kingsley name comes from an old English term. The "king's lea" described an area of forest and meadow set aside for sport hunting by the British king and his royal court. The royal gamekeepers used the king's lea to hunt wild game for the castle kitchen. Over many centuries the name has been spelled Chingeslie Kyngesleigh Kingesleigh Kingisley and Kingsley.

Kingsley Women

What are the stories of Kingsley wives and daughters in America? We know Elizabeth Kingsley's daughter Freedom had seven children with John French, who fell into disfavor with John Kingsley.

We can assume that some of the Kingsley wives died young of childbirth or disease or medical practice of the time. Their replacement wives raised Kingsley step-children along with their own new batch of Kingsley babies.

Household chores on the American frontier were exhaustive and never-ending for Kingsley mothers and for older daughters still at home. Yet they persevered.

For four centuries, from the 1600s to the 2000s, Kingsley women have moved ever westward. To Pennsylvania, Wisconsin, North Dakota, Colorado, California, Oregon.

Through most of Western history, women were biblically and legally required to submit to their husband's authority in all things. What about Kingsley women?

I like to think that John Kingsley's male descendants chose strong women to marry. Not to be submissive servants, but to be lifetime partners in a shared mission.

Indian Captive

Are you ready to J-U-M-P with me in time and space? Our destination is the Pennsylvania frontier. We are tracking down a family story. For two hundred years the Kingsleys in America have kept alive the story of Frances Kingsley, a young girl captured and raised by Indians in the 1700s.

Illustration from Harpers Weekly

Here's how the story goes. In the year 1778 Nathanial Kingsley was away from his family and farm as a soldier in the Revolutionary War. One day Nathanial's wife Rebeckah heard gunshots, a commotion, and ran outside the farmhouse, carrying her baby. Mrs. Kingsley was horrified to see her oldest boy being scalped by Indians. Her two other sons were being carried away as captives.

One of Mrs. Kingsley's sons had a lame leg. She begged the Indians to leave the crippled son and take her daughter Frances instead. So the Indians took seven-year-old Frances and the other son.

Many years later, Frances Kingsley found her way back to the Kingsley farm in Pennsylvania. Frances told the family she had been raised as a captive and she had married an Indian chief. Her brother had died in the Indian camp some years after their capture.

The Real Captive

The story of Frances Kingsley, Indian captive, is fascinating. But the story is not true, repeat, NOT TRUE. There was no Frances Kingsley. Instead, a neighbor girl Frances Slocum was captured and raised by Indians.

You might say the real Frances was captured twice. First by the Indians. Then mistakenly re-named a Kingsley and captured into Kingsley family lore for the next two hundred and fifty years.

Let me report here a more truthful account of the Kingsley and Slocum families as described in several books about Frances Slocum's life.

The story begins with Nathanial Kingsley 1744-1822, a grandson of ancestor John Kingsley 1635. Nathanial had settled with his family in the Susquehanna River Valley in eastern Pennsylvania. Nathanial farmed and he also soldiered in the Revolutionary War.

In 1778 Indian wars and bloody raids broke out across the Susquehanna Valley. Over 300 American settlers were killed by British forces and Seneca warriors.

Nathanial Kingsley was captured in battle and taken to Canada. At a nearby farm, Nathanial's neighbors Ruth and Jonathan Slocum had escaped the Indian raid. Nathanial Kingsley's sons Nathan age 14 and Windham age 10 were sent to stay with the Slocum family.

One day while Jonathan Slocum was away, three Indian warriors attacked the Slocum farm. Young Nathan Kingsley was outside sharpening a knife at a grinding stone. Nathan was wearing his father Nathanial's Revolutionary War jacket.

The sight of the military jacket enraged the Indians. They shot the Kingsley boy dead and scalped him with the knife the boy had been sharpening at the grindstone. The warriors then seized the two younger boys, Ebenezer Slocum and Windham Kingsley, as captives.

Ruth Slocum came out from her hiding place and pleaded with the Indians not to take her son Ebenezer because he was lame. So the Indians carried off Windham Kingsley age ten and Ruth's daughter Frances Slocum age five.

Maconnaquah

Frances Slocum was a beautiful little girl with long auburn hair. She was highly prized in the Indian settlement.

But young Windham Kingsley age ten was soon traded into another tribe. His fate was lost to history.

Frances was adopted and raised by a childless Indian couple of the tribe. They named her Maconnaquah "Little Bear."

As a young woman Maconnaquah married the tribal chief and had four children. She loved her family and her adopted people. In later life Maconnaquah was a respected widow of a great chief. Meanwhile the Slocum family in Pennsylvania never stopped their search for Frances.

Sixty years after Frances Slocum's capture, in 1835, an Indian trader discovered an elderly white woman living in an Indian lodge in Indiana. The woman told the agent a few fragments of what she remembered of English words and her former Slocum family.

Soon newspapers around the country reported that a white woman named Frances had been taken by the Indians when she was very young.

Frances Slocum's brothers found their long-lost sister in Indiana in 1837. They wanted to take their sister back to her childhood home in Wilkes-Barr, Pennsylvania. But Frances, known as Maconnaquah, chose to stay with her grown children and her adopted tribe in Indiana.

The historic accounts of Frances Slocum barely mention Nathanial Kingsley and his sons Nathan and Windham. Meanwhile the states of Indiana and Pennsylvania have historic monuments, parks and public schools named in honor of the Indian captive Frances Slocum.

Bishop Calvin Kingsley

Now we J-U-M-P in time and space to another descendant of John Kingsley with another connection to American Indians. Calvin Kingsley 1812-1870 was educated in Pennsylvania and became a bishop and influential leader in the Methodist Episcopal Church.

Illustration of Bishop Calvin Kingsley from Harpers Weekly 1870

Calvin Kingsley probably knew the tragic story of Nathanial Kingsley and his sons Nathan and Windham. Bishop Kingsley became editor of The Western Christian Advocate, a widely read newspaper in the 1800s.

Bishop Kingsley fervently believed that all Indians must be eradicated. He wrote in The Advocate, "What shall be done with the Africans and the Indians? There is no reason why an ignorant savage should be allowed land enough for hunting ground (that could) sustain a thousand civilized and Christianized persons."

Bishop Kingsley's impassioned editorials inspired two prominent Methodists of Colorado, Governor John Evans and Colonel John Chivington.

In November 1864 Colonel John Chivington led his volunteer regiment to an encampment of Cheyenne and Arapahoe Indians on the Colorado high plains. In an attack known as The Sand Creek Massacre, Chivington ordered his troops to kill every Indian in the camp.

The victims were mostly women, children and old men. Chivington ignored a white flag hoisted by tribal members. A few of Chivington's soldiers refused to carry out his orders.

Bishop Calvin Kingsley learned about the Sand Creek Massacre. In his Western Christian Advocate newspaper, Bishop Kingsley urged even more bloodshed. "Our only hope ... lies in the repetition of like battles. These Indians ... need occasional chastising."

The Mayflower

There is a Kingsley connection with two families who sailed the Mayflower in 1622. In the 1700s the descendants of John Billington and Stephen Hopkins married descendants of John Kingsley. Both men, Billington and Hopkins, were not Pilgrims, but were outsiders who booked passage on the same ship as the Pilgrims.

During the 1622 voyage John Billington and both his sons were known as troublemakers. As the Mayflower lay anchored in Provincetown Harbor, John Billington Junior fired off a musket on the ship's deck just for fun.

The shot nearly ignited an open keg of gunpowder. The men of the Mayflower were outraged that young Billington's prank could have sunk the ship before it landed at Plymouth.

John Billington Senior made his own kind of trouble. During the first months of settlement, Billington made "profane objections" to leader Miles Standish. Billington's actions got him arrested and sentenced to be tied to a post in the Plymouth public square.

John Billington Senior continued to make history when he argued with his neighbor and later shot the man dead. Billington was arrested again. He declared that the colonial court did not have the power to execute him for a capital offense.

But the men of the General Court were not persuaded. Our Mayflower ancestor John Billington was hanged for murder in 1630.

Our second Mayflower ancestor, Stephen Hopkins, had sailed to Bermuda thirteen years before his Mayflower voyage. During Stephen Hopkins' earlier voyage to Bermuda, he and his shipmates attempted a mutiny. When they reached Bermuda the rebellious sailors were arrested and sentenced to hang. Stephen Hopkins was given a last minute reprieve.

Some years later, with wife and children, Stephen Hopkins booked passage on the Mayflower. So history tells us that our Mayflower ancestors Hopkins and Billington both faced a date with the hangman. Billington lost, while Stephen Hopkins turned his life around.

In the new Plymouth Bay colony, Stephen Hopkins helped negotiate with the nearby Indians to keep the peace and to barter with the Indians for food. Even so, the colonists faced a hard winter of starvation and disease.

By spring half the Mayflower colonists who had originally arrived were dead. But both the Stephen Hopkins and John Billington families survived, with six living children among them. Their descendants married into Kingsley families in the 1700s.

Black And White

We know that John Kingsley boarded a ship for the colonies in 1635. We also know that other ships carried passengers to America in the same year. Why don't we try to J-U-M-P in time and space to John Kingsley's ship.

But what if we lose our way and land on a different ship altogether? What if we jump and then land on a slave ship bound for America? In an instant we become captured Africans, not free Englishmen. What if?

In the ship's dark hold we groan and weep in our iron shackles. We choke in the stench. Our fateful J-U-M-P onto the wrong ship binds us to the twelve million captured Africans who came to America between the years of 1619 and 1830.

With only a slight shift of European DNA to African DNA, we are now trapped into slavery, mother to child, for the next 230 years. We find outselves living a nightmare with no escape.

Slaves have no ancestor stories. Our slave owners demand a lifetime of labor in plantation fields. A few of us might be lucky enough to become house slaves or stable slaves or learn a useful skill. We can be beaten, bought, sold, inherited, mortgaged. We cannot marry, travel, earn money, or learn to read and write.

Each of us is born into lifelong slavery, even if some of us look like our white slave owner or his white teenage sons. We live in rough cabins behind the owner's mansion. The plantation ledger records our age and sex but not our names.

American slavery was the law of the land from the 1600s until the Emancipation Act of 1868. The Civil War ended slavery. But Southern white supremacy was enforced by the Ku Klux Klan and midnight lynchings.

Black history was not part of learned American history. Students might learn that slavery was tolerated for a few decades and that slaves were mostly well treated and content.

Zephaniah

Why write about blacks in America? Our Kingsley story has nothing to do with slavery. But why not ask the question. Did any Kingsleys own slaves?

I invite you to J-U-M-P with me in time and space to Fort George Island, Florida. There we find a historic site managed by the United States National Park Service. We are on the grounds of The Kingsley Plantation, owned by Zephaniah Kingsley 1765-1843.

We know that Zephaniah could not have been a descendant of our ancestor 1635 John Kingsley. Even so, the story of Zephaniah is worth the telling.

Zephaniah Kingsley was a Quaker from Bristol, England. Zephaniah became the captain of an English slave ship. He soon became a wealthy man. He purchased a fleet of schooners that he used to transport slaves to American plantations. With his immense profits he purchased a Florida plantation along with its 200 slaves.

Anna

Now we meet Anna Kingsley 1793–1870. Anna began her life in Africa as a beautiful Senegalese princess. In 1806 she was stolen by slave traders. At age 13 Anna was bought by Zephaniah Kingsley, who was then age 41. Anna became the first of Zephaniah's African wives.

As a Florida plantation owner Zephaniah strongly defended his right to own slaves and his right to keep several enslaved child "wives." Zephaniah never married a white woman.

Anna Kingsley and her African co-wives and their eleven slave children were Zephaniah's only family in America. Zephaniah granted Anna her freedom after she had three of his children. Anna had reached the age of twenty and had become too old for Zephaniah.

Today Zephaniah Kingsley would be arrested, tried, convicted and sentenced for sex trafficking, rape, sexual exploitation of minors and other offenses. But before the Civil War everything Zephaniah Kingsley did was perfectly legal in America.

Zephaniah's Florida plantation is now an official historic site managed by the United States National Park Service. A coastal road and bridge takes you to the island, with its stately plantation house and twenty-five slave cabins. Interpretive signs tell the story of Zephaniah and Anna Kingsley.

Battle Line

We cannot avoid the next J-U-M-P into the chaos of a Civil War battlefield. My great-grandfather Edward E Kingsley 1855-1934 was seven years old when his older brother Jefferson went to war. Jefferson Kingsley was a Wisconsin farm boy and skilled rifleman who joined the 18th Infantry Company K as a Union soldier. Jefferson fought his first major battle at Shiloh in western Tennessee.

The young soldier Jefferson likely carried a muzzle-loading one-shot rifle. This newer style of rifles had a range of 250 yards that could reach a target twice as far as the earlier muskets of the 1770s. But all the Civil War commanders of both North and South did not change their Revolutionary War battle line tactics. And so rows and rows of soldiers were mowed down by rifle fire. In battle after battle.

On April 6, 1862 Jefferson's father Edward W Kingsley was plowing his Wisconsin farm field when he stopped his team of horses, walked to the farmhouse, and announced, "Jefferson has been shot and killed." The father's premonition was deadly right.

Jefferson Kingsley was the oldest of Edward's fifteen children. Jefferson was killed on his first day of battle, one of 23,000 soldiers dead or wounded at the Battle of Shiloh. The young soldier did not live to fight another battle or to know the Union victory in 1864.

CHAPTER 4   WESTWARD

Edward And Christina

Now our trampoline of space and time takes us to my great-grandparents Edward E Kingsley 1855-1934 and Christina Anderson Kingsley 1858-1939. Edward and Christina raised seven daughters and three sons. We J-U-M-P to the rich farmlands and bonanza wheat fields of eastern North Dakota.

The Kingsley farmstead was close to the town of Wheatland, an easy walk to school for the ten children. By 1900 Wheatland was a prosperous settlement along the Great Northern rail line, with mercantiles, liveries, a hotel, school, churches and saloons.

Edward E Kingsley early 1930s

photo from Ronald A Kingsley

In 1905 the Wheatland Eagle newspaper reported that Edward Kingsley's barn and two granaries burned to the ground in a great fire. Neighbors rushed to help Edward save the farmhouse and all the livestock.

The Wheatland Eagle reported, "As a result of fright caused by the fire, Mrs. Kingsley was very ill for a time." At the time of the fire Christina Kingsley was raising their ten children at the farm home.

Edward E and Christina Kingsley family, about 1906

Back row: Laura, Fred, Clara, Walter, Caroline, Elizabeth (Lizzie)

Front row: Mabel, Edward E, Alice, Christina, Wallace, Edith.

In another story, the Wheatland Eagle reported that the oldest Kingsley son, Fred, accidentally shot his brother Walter. Christina Kingsley saved young Walter's life when she tightly bandaged his shattered arm, hitched horse to wagon and rushed him to town. Two doctors in Wheatland amputated Walter's arm. He was ten years old.

Many years later, Walter's older brother Fred lost an arm in a farm accident. Both Kingsley brothers, Fred and Walter, became skilled at operating and repairing farm machinery using one arm, not two. Since 1900, farm accidents have brought injury, death and heartache to a number of Kingsley households in the Wheatland community.

Lizzie And George

Now we pull on dusty cowboy boots and J-U-M-P even further west. The time is 1910 and we are looking for one of the seven daughters of Edward and Christina Kingsley. Lizzie (Elizabeth) Kingsley 1890-1966 married at age eighteen and moved away forever from her North Dakota farm.

Lizzie and her new husband George Colleps settled into their honeymoon homestead in the Rocky Mountains at Eagle, Colorado. Lizzie missed her Kingsley family. She sent them Kodak photograph cards of her life on their mountain ranch, her favorite horse, a captured coyote.

After several high country winters, George and Lizzie packed their stock wagon and moved to the milder climate of western Colorado. Lizzie's husband George was a cattleman and cowboy all of his life.

In early summer George and other ranchers led long strings of cattle up narrow trails onto the Grand Mesa. In the fall they herded cattle back down to the Grand Valley, three thousand feet below.

George and Lizzie's Kannah Creek ranch sat on the lower slope of Grand Mesa. George and Lizzie had no children of their own, but they would have known all the children of the local ranches.

Lizzie had little time to be a horsewoman. At roundup time Lizzie and the other ranch women fed the hungry ranch hands. Steak, mashed potatoes, gravy, vegetables, and fruit pie. The noon feeding came with steaming cowboy coffee, good-hearted teasing, tall tales and rounds of laughter.

Cow Camp

Lizzie spent part of every summer on the Grand Mesa cow camps with other ranch families. Cow camps were clusters of rough log cabins in grassy meadows near a spring or creek. Women cooked up meals from provisions carried to the mesa top on pack horses. Biscuits and gravy, baked beans, canned peaches, canned milk and cowboy coffee.

Children of the cow camps rode horses, worked and played through long summer days. Sometimes boys rode out with rifles to hunt deer and elk. They brought back dressed out quarters of meat on pack horses. Many years later one rancher's son declared that every September he left cow camp in tears. He wanted to stay forever on the Grand Mesa.

Cow camp on Grand Mesa, Colorado. Oil painting by the author

At branding time several Kannah Creek outfits joined up at a Grand Mesa cow camp. George and other cowboys flushed cattle and calves out of the trees, driving them to the "gather grounds." Cow camp children joined the roundup on their favorite horses. After dark a few cowboys and cow dogs took night watch with the agitated herd to prevent breakouts.

Branding started at daylight. Two ropers rode into the herd, looped a calf's leg and dragged the bawling calf to the branding station. Two men grabbed the calf, flipped it and held it down while another man branded with a red-hot iron. In a second the calf was up and running for its mama.

Saddle Up

In the fall season George and other ranchers gathered the herds to sort cattle by brands. Ranchers sorted out breeding stock to keep over for winter feeding and spring calving. The rest of the cows, yearlings and steers were herded to railroad yards at Whitewater in the Grand Valley, then loaded onto cattle cars bound for Denver.

Through the summer George rode his cow horse, sometimes fifty miles in a day. George was thrown off his horse and laid up more than a few times. Ranch work could bring on broken bones, frostbite, heat collapse, snake bite, or bloody wounds from ax or pitchfork. Lizzie and other ranch wives patched up the cowboys as best they could, far from doctor's care.

By age sixty, George's cowpunching days were over. George and Lizzie retired to a little house in Whitewater, Colorado. One time George brought out his saddle, chaps and spurs to show to my cousin Larry Murray. George wiped tears from his eyes and moustache as he shared stories about his ranching days and his beloved cow horse.

Range Wars

Long before George and Lizzie's time, the winter camps of the native Utes were cleared out and replaced by the thriving towns of Delta and Whitewater. Ranchers brought in vast herds of cattle and sheep. Cattle ranchers despised sheep ranchers. Sometimes masked cattlemen would shoot up an entire sheep herd during a night raid.

After the range wars came the water wars. The winter snowpack on Grand Mesa was the main water source for valley hayfields and orchards. In early years, irrigation disputes were settled by fist, shovel, pitchfork, or revolver.

Some places were named for the lawless era. Condemn It Park, Holy Terror Creek, Hell and Brimstone Corner. The cattle and sheep wars ended when federal grazing laws were passed in Congress. Water disputes ended when orchard growers organized their own self-governing water company.

Escalante Canyon

George and Lizzie knew all the stories about early-day ranch life in the grassy bottomlands of Escalante Canyon. The canyon cut deep into the sideslope of the Uncompahgre Plateau to the west of the Grand Mesa. The only way into Escalante Canyon was Big Hill, an old Ute horse trail with a six hundred foot drop from plateau to canyon bottom.

The first settlers used pack mules to transport lumber and machinery to their homesteads. A few farmers tried to widen the trail with picks and shovels.

In the 1890s one rancher led his new bride down the steep hairpin turns of Big Hill. For five years after, his bride refused to leave the canyon. By George and Lizzie's time the Big Hill road was improved enough for a Ford Model T.

Mc Carty Gang

The Grand Valley town of Delta claimed its own stories of the Old West. George and Lizzie knew all about the bank heist of 1893 when the McCarty gang robbed the Farmers and Merchants Bank of Delta. The robbery went bad when Fred McCarty fatally shot the bank cashier.

Across the street at the hardware store Ray Simpson heard gunfire and grabbed his ought-fifty caliber Sharps rifle. Simpson ran outside and saw three bank robbers galloping down Main Street.

Ray Simpson took aim and put a bullet in Bill McCarty's head. Fred McCarty saw his brother fall, reeled his horse and fired three shots at Simpson as Simpson reloaded. Fred missed all three shots. Simpson fired again and killed Fred McCarty.

Tom McCarty fled the town and then fled the state. Bill and Fred McCarty's corpses were displayed side by side on the Main Street of Delta. Ray Simpson, the hardware store owner and sharpshooter, became the town hero for all time.

Ben Lowe

George and Lizzie knew the story of Ben Lowe and Cash Sampson of Escalante Canyon. In the early 1900s the young rancher Ben Lowe was known as a showman, horse trader, and outlaw. Ben would coax his horse named Cloud to jump from the Escalante Canyon rim across a six foot gap to a formation called Table Rock.

Table Rock in Escalante Canyon, Colorado

photo by the author

He would steady Cloud and wave his hat to spectators below. No other horseman and no other horse ever attempted to jump the gap since Ben Lowe and Cloud.

Ben's best trick at local rodeos was to gallop his horse at top speed, lean down and shoot at a target from under the horse's neck.

Ben liked to bring fresh beef quarters to grateful hardscrabble families of Escalante Canyon. But the butchered meat did not come from Ben's brand.

Ben Lowe was known to lawmen as a horse stealing, cattle rustling outlaw. Ben sometimes had to escape to his stone shelter hidden away in the far end of the canyon.

Meanwhile Cash Sampson of Delta was a brand inspector, former county sheriff and a United States Marshal. Cash Sampson disliked cattle rustlers and horse thieves. Cash moved to a small ranch in Escalante Canyon so he could keep a closer eye on Ben Lowe.

One summer day in 1917 Cash stopped by the Musser ranch to see Kel and Eda Musser. Ben Lowe and his sons Willie and Bobby, ages eleven and nine, were at the Musser ranch house too. Ben and both his sons wore holsters with handguns.

The Lowes and Cash Sampson sat down to a noon dinner of beef stew and apple pie. Kel Musser said the conversation was polite, even though all four of their guests happened to be armed.

Shootout

After the meal Ben Lowe and his boys saddled up. Ben told them, "Go on ahead, I'll wait for Cash." So Willie and Bobby rode on down the trail. Soon the boys heard loud quarreling and then four shots. They turned their horses and raced back. Cash Sampson lay on the ground with a bullet through his head. Ben Lowe lay dying as blood filled his lungs.

Willie galloped his horse back to the Musser ranch and yelled, "Dad and Cash killed each other." Local ranchers gathered at the scene. There were no witnesses. There was no one left alive to be charged with murder. Cash took two bullets to his head and leg. A third shot from Ben's gun missed. Cash Sampson had shot Ben Lowe through the full length of Ben's torso.

The ranchers figured that Ben the showman had fired his trick shots from under the horse's neck. Cash saw the trick coming and fired back.

Rancher friends of Ben and Cash loaded their bodies into a wagon bed, side by side and covered with canvas. Then came the long slow journey down the canyon to the Delta coroner.

Today, in 2025, from our home on Cedar Mesa I can see the morning sun light up the golden sandstone escarpments of Escalante Canyon. The canyon emerges from the long skyline of the Uncompahgre Plateau west of Grand Mesa.

My husband Alex and I have explored Escalante Canyon by SUV, jeep and all-terrain vehicle. We've joined friends of our local archaeology chapter to hike to Ute rock art panels on Escalante Canyon walls.

The name Ben Lowe is carved into the canyon wall in the shade of cottonwood trees near an old corral. High on the cliff wall beside Table Rock is Ben Lowe's cattle brand etched into the wall with bullet holes.

Four Generations

Lizzie and George retired from Colorado ranch life in the 1950s. Several of Lizzie's Kingsley family traveled to Lizzie and George's 50th wedding anniversary in 1958. I was eleven years old when my Murray family piled into in our 1956 Pontiac for our one and only family road trip.

My father Roy Murray, my brother Roy Allan and Uncle Fred Kingsley rode the front bench seat. My mother Helen Murray and three children crowded into the back. No seat belts in those days. My older brother Noel, age fifteen, stayed behind to manage the farm, the dairy herd and all the summer fieldwork on his own.

Western Colorado has been home to four generations of Kingsley descendants: ranchers George and Lizzie, the Murrays of Delta and then my own family. From the town of Delta, my

Uncle Ray and Aunt Frieda Murray explored the southwest in their little four-seater airplane, a Mooney Ranger.

When Alex and I visited them one time in 1970 Uncle Ray said, "It's a nice day, let's fly out to the Grand Canyon and have a picnic." And so we did.

One time my grandmother Caroline Kingsley Murray traveled to her sister Lizzie's Kannah Creek ranch. Caroline's son Ray Murray of Delta decided to take his mother for a scenic mountain drive.

All her life Grandma Caroline had only known flat prairie land. The road twisted and climbed high into the San Juan Mountains. There were vertical granite walls, steep dropoffs and no guardrails.

The San Juan Mountains of Colorado

photo by the author

Grandma Caroline was afraid to look out the car windows. She crouched down on the floorboards of the car, whimpering and moaning until she was safely back in the Delta valley.

Today Grandma Caroline's descendants, myself and my family, navigate the San Juan Mountains on highways, jeep trails, all-terrain-vehicle trails and hiking trails. Our favorite is Corkscrew Gulch Trail outside of Ouray that climbs to Hurricane Pass at 12,700 feet.

Cedar Mesa

Since the year 2002 my husband Alex and I have lived on the edge of Cedar Mesa near Cedaredge, Colorado. We watch cloud shadows and sunlight move across the slopes of Grand Mesa. We share our Cedar Mesa acres with local wildlife. Fox, coyote, bobcat, bear, deer, and elk. Ravens and crows, hawks, eagles, blue jays, magpies and songbirds.

All around us are mountain ranges, mesas and valleys. To the west and north is towering Grand Mesa with its two thousand square miles of spruce forest, aspen and lakes.

Alex and his buddies explore miles of snowmobile and all-terrain-vehicle trails on public lands managed by the Forest Service. They stop to enjoy the views of the Uncompahgre Plateau, West Elks, San Juans, and La Sal Mountains. Alex and I take visitors to our nearby national parks - Black Canyon, Canyonlands and Arches.

After spring snowmelt Alex and I head for the high country in our pickup camper. In the fall we camp in groves of golden aspen. We hear bawling cattle, barking cow dogs and "Hi – Yea-ah, Hi – Ye-ah." Ranchers on horseback are herding cattle off the mesa, just like my Uncle George and his cow horse one hundred years ago.

Uteland

Western Colorado was the land of Native American Utes before their forced removal to reservation land. Alex and I joined the Colorado Archaeological Society. With other chapter members we explored the prehistory of western Colorado, Utah and New Mexico. We enrolled in archaeology classes.

We volunteered in archaeological surveys and field work on public lands that were once Ute lands. Across the southwest we have explored rock shelters, rock art, wikiups, ancestral Puebloan villages and cliff dwellings.

Ute winter camp, oil painting by the author

CHAPTER 5 JOHN AND CAROLINE

A Different Perspective

Many family histories tell stories of prosperity, successful public life and good fortune. The difficult stories are left out. Native Americans of the Southwest have a different perspective. Pueblo elders tell stories of failure and success in equal measure.

If a Zuni man is ashamed that he let his pickup truck roll into an arroyo, his people tell him stories of similar misfortune that happened to other Puebloans. The Zuni man is reassured that despite his mistake or personal disaster, he can persevere and move on.

We will share difficult family stories like the Puebloan people do. We will J-U-M-P back in time only a hundred years to the lives of my grandparents John Murray 1896 - 1950 and Caroline Kingsley Murray 1895 - 1985. I remember well my good-hearted Grandma Caroline. Her faded aprons, homemade bread and chokecherry jam.

I never knew my grandfather John Murray who died in his mid-fifties. My grandfather was not spoken of in our Methodist household. We children only knew of him as a drunken Irishman and poor provider for his family.

Shotgun Wedding

Here now is John and Caroline's story. John Murray was 17 and Caroline Kingsley was 18 when she became pregnant. Caroline's parents Edward and Christina Kingsley learned of the young couple's pregnancy. Edward and his older sons paid young John Murray a visit.

By fist or shotgun they persuaded John to take manly responsibility and marry Caroline. John and Caroline's marriage certificate of December 1914 included a physician affidavit declaring that John Murray was not feeble-minded, insane, or afflicted with venereal disease.

Troubles

John and Caroline's first child Raymond was born that spring within the bonds of holy matrimony. Time went by. John Murray found himself with a wife and six children to support by age twenty-five. John escaped whenever he could to the friendly taverns of their little town of Casselton in eastern North Dakota.

One time Caroline visited her parents Edward and Christina Kingsley at their Wheatland farm. The Kingsley family couldn't help but notice Caroline's bruises. Soon Caroline's brothers Fred and Walter paid a visit to John Murray. John was persuaded to never, ever think of beating his wife again.

Caroline could barely manage her many pregnancies and babies, so she asked her Kingsley sisters for help. That is how Mabel Kingsley Lauritsen came to raise Caroline's baby Roy, who became my father.

As a boy of eight Roy Murray learned that his aunt Caroline was his "real" mother, and Caroline had asked for him back. Little Roy begged to stay with his Ma and Pa Lauritsen's family.

Meanwhile John Murray, the reluctant head of household, expected his sons to leave school at eighth grade and earn their keep picking potatoes. The Murray boys left home to live with their Uncle Walt Kingsley so they could finish high school in Wheatland. The Murray girls left home as soon as they were able.

Caroline Kingsley Murray sometimes worked at a Casselton hotel. She hired a neighbor girl to help with housework and gardening. One day in 1939 the hired girl came to Caroline and John's door. She was carrying a newborn baby. "You're the father," she said to John Murray, "You raise him."

Caroline decided to raise baby boy Lyle as her own. We Murray kids were told Lyle was a foster son. Lyle grew up. An army recruiter looked at Lyle's birth certificate. "It says here your name is Lyle Lambert, not Lyle Murray." No one had thought to tell␣Lyle his legal surname or his birth story.

Lyle Lambert went on to serve in the military, marry, and move to Oregon. Lyle Lambert and his wife Freda raised four handsome sons in a loving family. After he retired Lyle donated his time and building skills to Habitat for Humanity.

I never knew my grandfather John Murray 1896 - 1950. Someone said he played the fiddle. Many of his tavern friends came to his funeral.

I never knew the young woman who gave up her beautiful baby boy to John and Caroline. Grandma Caroline's little house in Casselton was only seven miles from my family's Wheatland farm. But some family stories stay hidden.

As an adult my father Roy Murray needed a birth certificate but he had none. No one had remembered or written down or celebrated his birth day, so Roy had to make up a date of birth.

When I was older I was curious about my Murray name. A few older relatives had compiled basic family histories. One said John Murray's father Joseph was born in Ireland. Joseph Murray came to Minnesota and married Mary Koeplin. One of their ten children was my grandfather John Murray.

Highland Clan

I wanted to research my Irish roots. Time to J-U-M-P once again on the trampoline of time and space. But what is happening? We fly past Ireland and we land in the misty moors of the Scottish Highlands. I learn that my Murray name has Scottish origin, not Irish.

We travel back in time to the 1200s when the name Malcolm Murray appears in Scotland's earliest written records. Malcolm Murray is a sheriff. There are many other Murrays. In the year 1297 Sir Andrew Murray fought for Scottish independence. In the 1300s Sir Walter Murray was Regent of Scotland before he was killed in battle.

So instead of a tarnished Murray name of ill repute, I've discovered a Murray Clan of valor and fame. By the 1600s the Highland Murrays were dukes and earls, lords and ladies. Murray strongholds included Bothwell Castle, Blair Castle, and Scone Palace.

The Murrays took up arms against rival clans and against the English devils. At the Battle of Culloden in 1706, Lord George Murray led 4000 Jacobite men against an English army.

Some of the Murrays moved south and became Englishmen. One was James Murray, who finished his life-long work in 1870 when he published the Oxford English Dictionary. Now digitalized, the OED is found in most libraries of the English-speaking world.

There is a Murray story of treachery and lechery. It goes like this. In 1697 Mungo Murray of Scone Palace was the Lord High Commissioner of the Church of Scotland. A feud broke out between the Murray Clan and the Fraiser Clan. Simon Fraiser, known as "Old Fox," ambushed and captured Mungo Murray at Scone Palace.

The "Old Fox" and his troops abducted and carried away Murray's young daughter. Mungo Murray's sons gathered 600 loyal clansmen to give chase. But Simon Fraiser escaped to the highlands and quickly arranged a marriage to Lord Mungo Murray's beautiful daughter.

So now we J-U-M-P forward in time to my own family of Murrays. We meet up with an American descendant of the Scottish Fraser Clan whose name is James Van Duyn. In the 1960s young James Van Duyn courted my sister Nedra Murray. They married in 1970.

And so history comes full circle as yet another man of the Fraser Clan cannot resist a charming young lady of the Murray Clan. James Van Duyn and Nedra Murray forged a happily-ever-after union a few centuries after "Old Fox" Simon Fraser carried off Lord Mungo Murray's daughter.

John Murray The Englishman

We Murray children only knew our grandfather John Murray as a scoundrel. I learned of another John Murray who was in America during the time of the Revolutionary War. But this Murray was on the side of the British, not the colonists.

In 1775 this other John Murray was the British Royal Governor of the Colony of Virginia. American colonists were protesting British control, the tax on tea and the hated British Stamp Act.

The British Royal Governor John Murray warned the colonists that if they didn't stop their rabble-rousing he would "declare Freedom to the Slaves." The Governor's threat to end slavery further inflamed landowners. They faced financial ruin if they lost their right to own slaves.

In 1776 Thomas Jefferson and the other colonists penned their passionate Declaration of Independence from British oppression.

What happened to the other John Murray? When the

Revolutionary War broke out, the British Royal Governor John Murray narrowly escaped with his life. He boarded a ship and high-tailed it back to England.

Highland Connection

In the early 2000s I wanted to visit the Scottish Highlands of the Murray Clan. My husband Alex and I joined my cousin Paula Murray Ball and Bud Ball of Oregon. Paula and I inspected the royal rooms and treasures of Blair Castle while Alex and Bud toured a nearby whiskey distillery.

Macgregor Clan

I found a curious Scottish Highland connection that crosses two centuries. There once was a Lady Elizabeth Murray of Blair Castle. In 1780 she married Sir Evan MacGregor.

The MacGregors of Scotland had endured a tragic history when their clan was outlawed in the 1550s. The MacGregor clan lost all their land. The clan chief Duncan MacGregor and his sons were beheaded.

But fortunes change, and by the 1700s the MacGregor clan regained their good name. Robert MacGregor, known as Rob Roy and Brave Heart, was immortalized in legend, ballads and Hollywood movies.

Now we fast-forward to the 1900s and another Murray - MacGregor connection. In 1956 my father Roy Murray acquired our family farm at Wheatland from the original homesteader, Murdo MacGregor and his son Duncan MacGregor.

Fearless

In the eight centuries of Scottish history and legend, only a few Murray women are ever mentioned. Where are their stories? Here I will tell of my aunt Frieda Murray who I knew like a mother.

Frieda was a woman of undaunted courage. In the 1940s she left Missouri for Colorado. When my uncle Ray Murray courted her, he told her their marriage would have to include his three small children from a previous marriage. Frieda said, "That would be a bonus."

At age 29 she said "I do." Frieda became Ray's wife and a new mother to Ed, Paula and Larry who were ages 6, 5 and 4. Ray and Frieda Murray began their lifelong love story.

In Delta, Colorado the Murrays lived in a tent while Ray built their first home. Frieda was a public school teacher. Ray and Frieda both became licensed pilots. Frieda said that landing their little plane on a small gravel runway was the scariest thing she'd ever done.

Lillies And John

My mother was Helen Hawkes Murray. In the 1980s a genealogy of the Hawkes family was compiled by Mary Dunstan of Burbank, California.

Now we J–U–M–P to a story about one of my ancestors, Isaac Sanford Hawkes 1817-1860 of Connecticut. When Isaac died in 1860 his wife Lillies Hopkins Hawkes became a widow with five young children. Lillies' oldest son Isaac Farmer Hawkes became man of the family at age 16.

One year after Isaac Sanford Hawkes died, Lillies married again. Her new husband was a young local farmer, John Quincy

Adams, who was named for a president. On their wedding day John Adams was 19 and Lillies Hawkes was 40.

We only know the most basic of facts. Why did John and Lillies marry? Did Lillies' son Isaac accept his new step-father? The newly married John Adams was not yet twenty years old when he moved into the household of a 40 year old widow and her five children.

The Civil War broke out one year after John and Lillies were married. John Adams quickly enlisted in the Union Army. When he left for the war Lillies was newly pregnant and with five other children.

John Adams never returned. He died of smallpox before the Civil War had ended. Lillies Hawkes Adams was now twice widowed. She lived a long life in Connecticut with her six children before she died in 1907.

Lillies' son Isaac Farmer Hawkes was born in 1844 in Providence, Rhode Island. Most of his descendants settled in western Canada. A few Hawkes proved up homesteads in North Dakota.

One was my grandfather Ezra Bernard Hawkes 1886 – 1977. He married my grandmother Adeline Koch Hawkes in 1913. My grandmother Adeline died of cancer before I was born.

My mother Helen Hawkes Murray 1916 – 1998 shared no stories about her childhood during the time of the Great Depression. She shared no stories about her years working as a housemaid in Chicago.

My mother Helen Hawkes met my father Roy Murray and married him in Chicago in 1941. Roy and Helen Murray returned to North Dakota to live and farm near the Kingsley farms.

Grain elevator, Absaraka North Dakota

oil painting by the author

CHAPTER 6   PRAIRIELAND

Puritan Ways

Our ancestor John Kingsley of 1635 would have approved of my family's Puritan ways in the 1950s. My father Roy Murray's staunch Methodism allowed for no extravagance, exuberance or merriment. No parental hugs, kisses, cuddles, not even a pat on the back.

Any physical contact between our father and mother was undercover or under covers, never seen by the children. No terms of endearment were ever said. "Sweetheart" "I love you" were never heard between our parents or from parents to children.

Once I merited a handshake from my father because, as school board president, he was required to shake hands with all of us graduating seniors on the stage. At a gathering of relatives after my high school graduation I remember the remarkable feeling of a hug from Grandma Caroline.

And there was a brief point of contact with my father's arm when he walked me down the aisle to give me away to my husband Alex on our wedding day.

I now realize how unhappy and trapped our mother must have felt as a farm wife in the 1950s. She seldom interacted with us children. We learned to stay out of her way in general fear of her angry flares of temper.

My parents lived a life of Christian service and duty. Farm work and milking chores came before any family outing. In our Methodist home there were no record players or popular music or comic books or any other books. The only approved town movies were The Ten Commandments and Ben Hur.

My father never smoked or drank or swore, and he never

stepped inside the sociable Wheatland tavern. Community scandals were not spoken of. National events and world events were never topics of supper conversation.

We attended Sunday sermons, Sunday school, youth fellowship, choir practice, summer bible school and church camps. My father and mother attended men's and women's service groups, bible study, prayer meetings and church board meetings.

My older brothers rebelled. Said they would rather shovel manure and catch up on farm chores on Sunday morning.

The supper meal began at six pm after milking chores. Eight of us crowded around the table. Mother and father, five children and the hired man. After grace, food was passed around the table.

A platter of meat, boiled potatoes, bland vegetable heated from a can, a stack of white bread, a milk pitcher from the barn.

Roy and Helen Murray family, Wheatland, North Dakota

Nedra, Laurie, Helen, Quentin, Roy, Allan, Noel in 1959

My family maintained a strict work ethic. In the summer my brothers Noel and Roy Allan worked dawn to dusk managing our dairy herd, planting and harvesting the crops.

My younger sister Nedra and I pitched in. We learned to milk cows and clean milking machines. We sometimes helped my brothers in the fields. We learned to plow, cultivate, bale hay, swath, drive grain trucks and operate the John Deer self-propelled combine.

We children endured long North Dakota winters followed by a few months of glorious summer sunshine.

Education

In 1952 my brothers and I attended a one-room country school with nine wood desks, an oil stove and an outhouse. My beloved teacher Mrs. Ford let me practice writing in cursive when I was five years old.

After our little school closed for good we attended town school in Wheatland. My teacher had a sharp, shrill voice and a moustache. She disliked children and forbade my cursive writing. Later, in the 1960s, our high school barely stayed open with two dozen students, four teachers, sports for boys and home economics for girls.

Laurie Murray and Alex Labak married 1967 in Moorhead Minnesota

Milestones

My happiest years began when I left home, attended college in Minnesota and married my beloved Alex.

We started our life together in a little cabin by a big lake near Detroit Lakes, Minnesota. Our Minnesota friends, four generations of the Faltersack family, helped us launch our married life.

When we were in our twenties Alex and I took turns working and going to school. Then we moved to Colorado, raised a family and made our own story.

Labak family in Colorado 1983 personal photo

Alex 1942, Alaina 1980, Andrea 1977

Laurie 1947, Aleta 1976, Robert 1979

CHAPTER 7 FIRST RESPONDER

Nine-One-One

In the 1990s I was a firefighter and emergency medical technician with our rural volunteer fire department in Colorado. Here I will share with you my own story.

Now J–U–M–P with me into a firetruck. Lights flash and sirens blare. Our firetruck crests a hill on a bitterly cold January night. In the distance we see a massive wooden barn fully engulfed in flames.

As we stream water onto the fire, a layer of treacherous ice builds up around our firetrucks and water tanker trucks. Later, in the cooling ashes our fire chief finds the source of the fire, a small gas heater. Then he finds footprints in the snow, the leaping steps of a vagrant lodger.

For ten years I was a first responder with our fire district team of volunteers. We responded to structure fires, wildfires, industrial accidents, car crashes. Our medical calls sometimes involved drug use, domestic abuse, workplace assaults, murders.

Louviers Volunteer Fire Department 1995

Major incidents were photographed, filmed and reported by local newspaper and television crews. Our district also served a nearby state park where we responded to brush fires, campsite emergencies, and injuries from boating, bicycling, and hot air balloons.

In one fire call, a resident reported her house filling with smoke, but she saw no flames. The fire chief and I suited up and entered the house with a charged water hose.

In a teenage boy's bedroom, we saw smoke coming out around a trap door entrance to a crawl space. Inside we could see a small line of flames on the dirt floor. The fire chief directed me to crawl through the trap door and put out the fire. So I did.

We found evidence that the teenage boy and his friend had been using the crawl space as a hideaway. Abandoned candles had ignited their Playboy magazine collection.

At another incident a garage fire had spread to the attic of the main house. Our rural fire district had no working fire hydrants. My job was to guide the water tanker trucks to our portable water tank.

By the next morning the garage was fully destroyed but the main house was saved. In the rubble of a covered breezeway, a full size blackened ceramic Buddha sat with a serene smile.

Another firefighter and I were the only responders to a report of smoke in the area. We located and extinguished a fire in a scrap wood pile. A countywide burn ban was in effect. The property owner was surprised to see an all-woman team of firefighters.

We joined firefighters from several districts at a wildfire in the foothills. A news helicopter landed nearby. Winds died down, the fire came under control, and the helicopter pilot asked if anyone would like a ride down the hill. I got to go.

There was no door to the helicopter so I buckled in and we rode over the treetops to the fire staging area far below.

At a night time incident, a geyser of flames shot high in the air from an oversized propane tank in an industrial park. Our fire chief set up incident command and issued assignments. To me, "You'll engineer."

Louviers Volunteer Fire Department 1990

Training photo by the author

In the back cab of our new firetruck, I operated the panel that controlled water supply coming in from two hoses and going out to six hoses. An array of controls set engine power level and valves to each of the hoses. Streams of water spray cooled the tank as the escaping fuel gradually burned off.

Emergency Medical Technician

At one of my first medical calls I sat with a distraught older couple while helicopter medics attended their adult son. The son had come to the home with a fresh pizza. His pickup truck started rolling as he was getting out. When he fell the truck rolled over his chest and stopped, suffocating him. The medics could not revive him.

At a farmyard the resident directed us to an ill and incoherent elderly man. The old man lived in a farm shed that smelled of urine and sickness and lack of basic care. The man in the farmhouse did not ask about our patient and did not follow the ambulance to the hospital.

A boy fell thirty feet from a tree. It was our address, and our own son Robert, age 11. He had been setting up a rope swing in a tall cottonwood tree. Robert's friend ran to our house for help. I ran to Robert.

Son Robert was conscious but groggy, with back pain. Our neighbor came and I asked him to call 9-1-1. Our fire personnel arrived, strapped Robert onto a backboard and carried him uphill to the ambulance.

I rode with Robert to the hospital, thirty miles away. Robert had a concussion and several cracked vertebrae. Robert was flat on his back in the children's ward for four weeks. He didn't complain about having to miss a month of school.

One night a woman was reported walking along the highway. She was wet, cold and drunk. Her car had high-centered and stalled when she tried to drive along railroad tracks.

Then she stumbled into a water-filled canal, climbed out and tried to hitchhike. Meanwhile a Santa Fe freight train rammed her abandoned car. We treated the woman for hypothermia while Colorado highway patrol officers talked to her.

Impact

At a head-on collision on a two lane highway, the young woman driver sustained injuries despite her seat belt. In the back seat I tended to her wailing infant. The baby had been securely strapped into a child safety seat and was uninjured. At that time, child safety seats were a new requirement.

We responded to a rural crash scene on a warm summer night with bright stars close overhead. A new pickup truck had rolled several times at high speed and landed on its side in a field. The young male driver was dazed and staggering around.

We examined the young male passenger whose body had been thrown about twenty feet as the truck rolled. He was unresponsive with blood oozing from mouth, nose and ears.

I helped the paramedics with ambulance transport to the hospital. The emergency room staff worked for several hours before pronouncing death from serious brain trauma.

At another nighttime call, a tiny Volkswagon drove into the side of a fast-moving train at a railroad crossing. The VW was so lightweight that it bounced back off the moving train. The male driver was injured and his passenger was killed. The driver was drunk and never asked about his passenger.

At a medical call, a house painter was working alone on a third story ladder when he fell. He was knocked unconscious, woke up, then lay for several hours in extreme pain. Children getting off a school bus heard him yell for help.

On the scene, our EMTs stabilized the injured man with backboard, cervical collar and oxygen. The house painter suffered a concussion, broken pelvis and spinal injuries. We learned later that he needed several months of recovery and rehab before he could return to work.

Bad Luck

In an industrial area a giant yellow earthmover had run over a late-model Lexus sedan. When we saw the crushed car and the towering earthmover, we expected to find no survivors. Our firefighters used hydraulic "jaws of life" to pry up the top half of the Lexus.

Inside was a small-statured Asian man in suit and tie with no serious injuries. He'd had just enough time to crouch down as his well-built Lexus collapsed around him.

The man had driven past warning signs onto a large construction site. He said, "I honk my horn, I yell and I yell, but the big machine just kept backing up until he was on top of me."

Another emergency medical technician and I attended to the earthmover operator. He had suddenly collapsed from the summer heat and from his anxiety about the driver and crushed car. "I didn't hear him or see him," he said.

At an industrial park office on a Sunday morning, a woman was unconscious with a head laceration. The man who called 9-1-1 said his secretary had slipped and fallen.

The woman was wearing a short skirt and black fishnet stockings. An EMT confirmed that she was faking unconsciousness. Sheriff deputies were there to sort out the stories of the secretary and her boss that Sunday morning.

Our four patients came down from the sky in a hot air balloon at the nearby state park. Blustery winds had caused a collision with a picnic table. The riders were jostled and bruised but did not need ambulance transport.

My EMT certification required a ride-along shift with the Denver Ambulance Service. The two young men paramedics had good medical skills, but they never once changed the gurney sheet, pillowcase and blanket during five patient transports. A woman with a broken pelvis was placed onto the same bedding as a sick old man in his pajamas. I was disgusted.

Body Bags

One spring night we were dispatched to a major incident. A vehicle had erupted in flames after it was hit by a Santa Fe train at a crossing.

A witness reported he had seen the car leave a teenage keg party shortly before the crash. We put out the fire and started looking for victims.

Our fire chief asked me to use a tarp to cover the body of a teenage girl who had been ejected and lay about thirty feet from the car. The body of a teenage boy was in the driver's seat. His hand, burned to the bone, still gripped the steering wheel.

After impact with the train, the car had spun, rolled and landed on a secondary train track before it burst into flame. Underneath the car and between the rails was a third body. Ambulance medics arrived and radioed for additional body bags.

Two of our firefighters volunteered for a gruesome duty. They helped the paramedics remove three more bodies, burned and fused together, from the crushed back seat space of the vehicle.

from The Denver Post newspaper photo archives 1995

Six teenagers died in the crash. Reporters and television news crews arrived but were kept from the scene by highway patrol officers. The teenage driver was later found to have an extremely high blood alcohol level.

For several weeks after the car-train crash, grieving parents and students came to the scene of the crash to leave flowers and mementos.

Crime Spree

A morning 9-1-1 call came from the home of a retired couple. The elderly man reported that he, his wife and his daughter had all been shot.

Sheriff deputies and our fire chief entered the house to secure the scene. They confirmed the deaths of the wife and adult daughter while EMTs treated the husband's head wound.

Further events revealed that a young male gunman, high on crack cocaine, had launched a violent crime spree that included four homes in three counties. One woman was raped and seven people were shot.   Three people died, including the gunman.

The murderous spree was reported in newspapers and television news across the country.   The many victims and their families faced slow recoveries and shattered lives.

Hang It Up

My last year as a firefighter – emergency medical technician was 1997. Like many military families, each of our volunteer first responders had strong support from their families. I could not have served for ten years without the help of my husband Alex and our four children.

My fellow firefighters and EMTs became good friends. We worked well together, even under extreme conditions. Each of the 9-1-1 calls was a unique story of real people who needed immediate help.

The ranchlands of our rural fire protection district began to fill with suburban housing. A railroad overpass replaced the treacherous rail crossing. Our fire district was absorbed into a large metro fire department.

In the year 1999 the nearby Littleton community of Columbine High School endured a tragic morning of gunfire and mass killings. Then came the September 11, 2001 terrorist attack on the New York World Trade Center and the Pentagon.

The next year, 2002, Alex retired from Arapahoe Community College. We sold our house on the Front Range and moved west to beautiful, peaceful Cedaredge, Colorado.

CHAPTER 8   D - DAY

Drafted

My father-in-law, Alex Labak Sr, was known as Al Labak. Al served in the U.S. Army in four major campaigns of World War II. In 1986 I asked him to tell me about his wartime service so I could write it down. This is Al Labak's story. Now brace yourself as you J-U-M-P with me onto the beaches of Normandy June 6, 1944.

Al was drafted into the U.S. Army in 1942. He had to leave Stella, his pregnant wife, and a good job. Al trained for the army artillery. Al shipped to Europe in April 1944 on the Queen Elizabeth I.

"We were 16,500 men, 1500 nurses, and all of our battlefield equipment." The ship maintained a zigzag course to evade German U2 submarines. Al was given food twice a day during the six day crossing.

The ship anchored in the English coastal town of Bournemouth. The marshalling area was packed with hundreds of thousands of soldiers and miles of jeeps. Ships were docked along the coast end to end for seventeen miles.

Al said, "No one knew the precise date for the invasion." Al stayed with his jeep and waterproofed it with cosmolene, a substance like modeling clay. The exhaust pipe of his jeep stuck straight up to survive a water landing.

Normandy

In early June 1944 Al's First Army got their order from General Eisenhower, "GO." Under cover of dark, thousands of soldiers loaded onto ships.

Al said, "I drove my jeep onto a net basket. Jeep and driver were picked up by a crane, swung over the ship's hold and lowered down." The ship launched as soon as it was loaded.

Then a bad storm hit. The ship pitched and rolled. The crowded decks were soon covered with pools of vomit. All the ships were ordered back to England. The foiled operation helped prepare the troops for the final attempt.

June 6, 1944 was D-Day. All ships headed for the beaches of Normandy, France. The landing came in six main waves lasting until late afternoon. That first day 150,000 men landed. There were 10,000 casualties.

Al was not part of the first assault that sustained the biggest slaughter. The ship carrying Al's artillery battery arrived just after the beachhead was established.

"Our ship anchored about half a mile from the Normandy beach." Al drove his jeep onto the net basket. He and the jeep were hoisted up and dropped into an LST, or Tank Landing Ship.

The LST was quickly loaded with Al's entire artillery battery and equipment. The LST anchored close to shore. Al's First Sergeant told the jeep drivers, "When the LST drops the gate, GO, and GO like HELL!"

They all started their jeeps. "When the gate dropped I saw the beaches and cliffs of Normandy."

In part of an unending line, Al drove his jeep off the gate into waist deep water and then onto the sandy beach. Hundreds of LSTs unloaded GIs and equipment at the Normandy beach, with U.S. aircraft providing cover.

The choice of Normandy for the invasion caught the Germans by surprise. Even so, the Germans had been building up defenses for months.

The first GIs to arrive were silent glider pilots and paratroopers, but many of them were slaughtered. The next wave of GIs landed under heavy German fire from concrete bunkers on the cliffs above Normandy beach.

Bulldozers pushed dead bodies of soldiers into piles to clear pathways for later waves of landing GIs. The GIs from earliest landings had to scale the cliffs under enemy fire to set charges and bomb the concrete bunkers.

As soon as part of the cliff was blasted out, army engineers built a road up the cliff sides. Only then could shiploads of troops move off the beaches and onto the mainland.

Al's First Sergeant led the battalion vehicles up the narrow cliff road as darkness set in. Al's battalion was continually getting shells from German artillery.

Their stopping point was the site of a big battle earlier in the day. All around them were dead GIs and the stench of burning tanks, dead bodies and dead livestock. The First Sergeant's orders, "Dig in. Slit trench."

In the dark, Al dug a coffin-sized trench with his small spade. Al slept in the trench until morning. Front lines were not yet established.

Al said, "During the first five days all was confusion as our artillery battery moved around." Chow line rations shrank to twelve beans and one slice of bread per plate.

Howitzers

Al described how his artillery battalion operated. The headquarters of the artillery battery calculated the logistics for firing the howitzers. Ammo was supplied by huge ammunition dumps that stored firing powder in railroad cars. Trucks transported shells from the ammo dump to the artillery position.

Howitzer and artillery gunners

photo from WWII military archive

Cannoneers used cranes to move each shell to a "stretcher" and then to the back of a gun. The cannoneer inserted a radio timer. The howitzers fired 300-pound shells, and each shell held 80 pounds of gunpowder.

Four men lined up the 300-pound shell with the breech. Four other men used a ramrod to insert the gunpowder, then close and lock the breech.

In the artillery battalion, the First Sergeant assigned Al to be a jeep driver for a forward observer crew. Al described their operations.

The radio man in Al's jeep would report to a low-flying Piper Cub pilot that he'd sighted German tanks. Then the radio man ordered the artillery gunners to fire one round near the German tanks.

The Piper Cub above would observe and report how many degrees and yards away from the German tanks the first shell hit. The guns would then swivel into position to hit the targeted German tanks.

Al said, "The second firing never missed. The Germans couldn't figure out how our guns could hit targets from twenty miles away."

The rolling French farmland was divided by hedgerows. Al said, "We stopped at one place that looked like a landscape painting. There was a stream, an old flour mill and a waterwheel. A French woman was by the stream, washing clothes with a paddle."

But most of Normandy was a scarred battlefield with dead bodies, dead and bloated cattle and buzzing flies. Al got used to it.

"I once sat at a fallen tree and ate K-rations with the stench all around me." During many months of combat, Al was outdoors with no shelter, not even a barn or a chicken coop.

France

Now 26 divisions with 85,000 men were in France. One day Al's artillery battalion was given liberties. At a farmer's barn, the GIs found a huge oak barrel vat and spigot.

The barrel vat was filled with 500 gallons of calvadose, a 140-proof apple brandy made from rotting apples. Each jeep in the battery held two five-gallon water cans. By mid-morning every available water can was filled with calvadose.

At one p.m. Al's artillery battery was ordered to provide firing cover. But most of the GIs were drunk or passed out. Al did not say his own condition. "The Colonel was mad when he found out about the French apple brandy."

In July 1944 General Patton's Third Army was fighting the Battle of St. Lo and needed help from Eisenhower's First Army. Al described the First Army's actions.

After artillery guns softened a town with shells, an armored tank division plus infantry moved in. Infantry GIs, about fifteen men, would climb onto the back of a Sherman tank.

When the fast-moving Sherman tank was close to a town, soldiers leaped off the tank, scattered, and found shelter. The infantry GIs began drawing and returning fire to the holed-up German snipers. As soon as a town was captured, the next town became the objective.

The First Army was approaching Paris. The French pleaded, "Don't destroy our city." The Germans and Americans agreed there would be no firing on the city of Paris and the Germans would retreat. So Paris was never shelled.

Al's artillery battery moved on to Versailles, about ten miles south and west of Paris. It was Sunday afternoon when Al's outfit set up position. The GIs were ordered not to use any French facilities.

Al said, "Our latrine was a trench and a tarp for cover." They were stationed near the formal gardens and royal palace of Versailles. Their outfit was allowed no liberty.

Al's friend was a chauffeur for the Colonel. Al's friend said, "Let's sneak into Paris."

Six soldiers including Al crowded into the Colonel's Command Car, drove to Paris and rode down the Boulevard of the Arc de Triomphe. "The French civilians greeted us with cheers, dancing and champagne."

All the French people were celebrating Paris's liberation from the Germans. Al saw a few women with shaved heads. They had been caught collaborating with Germans. The GIs drove down Parisian parkways lined with small shops.

Al's group returned to their outfit near Versailles unnoticed. The next day the First Army was ordered to go around Paris, and soldiers were not allowed into the city.

War Zone

Al's artillery battery began to move east through Belgium in operation Battle Star. At the German border they ran up against the Siegfried Line with miles of jagged concrete and spikes.

German defenders hid behind small windows in concrete block houses, refusing to come out. General Eisenhower commanded the assault.

Armored bulldozers, supported by artillery from Al's battery, began pushing dirt up to the doors and windows and then over the tops of the concrete blockhouses. General Eisenhower's battalions passed over the Siegfried Line on the earthen bridges built by the Army Corps of Engineers.

Army jeep from WWII military photo archive

One time Al was alone in his jeep at a hedgerow crossing with no cover. He had orders to sit and wait. He took off his helmet and leaned against the radio equipment that filled the back of the jeep. In the sky overhead Al watched three American fighter planes in a dog fight with one German plane.

One of the American pilots hit the German plane. Al watched the plane come down in a dive, all the while firing machine guns. Bullets hit closer and closer.

Machine gun bullets hit the radio just behind Al's unprotected head. Then the German plane crashed a half mile from Al's jeep, exploding in a fireball.

Al's artillery battery was stationed at the town of Aachen at the border of Germany and Belgium. American aircraft and artillery had nearly leveled the town. American infantry "housecleaners" had cleared out snipers.

Army engineers with metal detectors had dug up thousands of landmine explosives and stacked them in piles along the road. Al's battery had to wait at Aachen because of a battle stalemate.

Some GIs saw the town's street car barn on a hill above town. The open streetcars had a long seat on each side. Al said, "Someone had an idea."

The GIs loaded a streetcar with landmines. They pushed the streetcar until it started rolling down the hill toward town. "When the streetcar hit a burned out truck, all the land mines blew up in a tremendous explosion."

Now it was September, 1944. Al's artillery battery was ten miles inside Germany. Their orders had been to not use anything belonging to French or Belgian civilians. For four months Al had slept outside.

In Germany their orders changed and they could now stay in German buildings. But Al's job as jeep driver kept him away from indoor quarters.

Al said, "My only personal items were a fountain pen and my army dog tags. I had no watch, not even a wallet."

Al owned two pairs of pants, a jacket, two shirts, a GI cap, an army helmet with wool liner, and two pairs each of socks, long johns and undershirts.

Out of Al's combat pay, he sent his wife Stella eighty dollars a month. "I kept nine dollars for life insurance, cigarettes and gambling."

Battle Of The Bulge

It was now getting toward Christmas 1944 and it was very cold. Al and his buddies thought the war would be over in a few weeks.

They were in Eschweiler, Germany, about 150 miles from Berlin. There was heavy combat all around.

The American forces stopped advancing. German General Von Ruchstadt broke through the American lines with his 65-ton armored Tiger tanks.

Al's battalion got a fifteen-minute march order. "It meant you have fifteen minutes to G-E-T O-U-T."

"We were in full retreat for 300 miles all the way back to Belgium." They were headed for the Battle of the Bulge in the Ardennes.

The convoy stopped to fuel their vehicles, do quick repairs and eat. They encountered a new German weapon called a buzz bomb.

The motorized bombs emitted a loud buzzing as they passed overhead, directed toward Liege, Belgium. Liege became "Buzz Bomb Alley."

The artillery battalion was now surrounded. The Germans knew the Americans were in the area. Battalion orders were, "No shelter and no fires."

The First Sergeant assigned Al to guard duty at a crossroad. Al was already chilled to the bone from eighteen hours of winter travel in an open jeep.

Al stood his four hour watch in extreme cold. He felt frozen. His cold wet feet became completely numb.

When the 6 a.m. relief guard came, Al stumbled back to his outfit. The First Sergeant said, "There's no place to warm up."

The skin and tissues of Al's feet were frozen. Al had no other work assignments, so he went to his jeep. He had two army blankets plus a long warm overcoat.

Al took off his boots. This was rare for a GI to do in the winter because with no shelter they wore their boots twenty-four hours a day. Al's toes were like brittle ice.

With his shoes off he slowly thawed his frozen feet by rubbing them with his hands. He wrapped a blanket over his feet, then hunkered down under the blanket and huffed warm air from his lungs to warm up his feet. Finally he slept.

Al said, "During the night it snowed an inch over my blankets, but my feet had thawed out."

Another time Al was on guard duty when he heard a great round of German artillery coming in. Al dived under a truck to avoid shrapnel. The bomb exploded only twenty yards from Al, making a crater large enough to bury a truck.

Gas Dump

Army engineers had laid a gas pipeline from the Normandy beach to the front lines. A temporary gas dump was near Al's outfit in Belgium. The gas dump held three million gallons of gasoline in five-gallon cans stacked like cordwood.

General Headquarters requested Al's outfit to get out the gas before the Germans overtook it. The First Sergeant picked Al along with seven others, plus four trucks.

Al said, "Every one of us felt doomed." Al partnered with Soupy and they reported to the gas dump in their 6x6 army truck.

A Second Lieutenant at the gas dump ordered them to load their truck with gas cans and drive to a safe area forty miles away and unload. It was wintertime with rough, icy roads. Their truck was equipped with a single skid chain on each wheel.

As fast as they could, Soupy and Al loaded 100 gas cans onto the truck, totaling 500 gallons of gas. After the forty-mile trip, they quickly unloaded the cans, then returned to the gas dump.

They made four trips. The work was a great strain on their backs and they became exhausted.

Army 6x6 truck from WWII military photo archive

During one of the trips their truck was coming down a steep hill with a full load of one hundred cans of sloshing gasoline. Suddenly the skid chain on one wheel snapped and started slapping on the road.

Al said, "I thought maybe we should stop the truck and take off the chain, but Soupy was driving and did not stop."

They were building up speed as they came down the hill. Far below, a local farmer in a horse-drawn wagon slowly started to cross the road.

Soupy tromped on the brake pedal, then shouted, "We haven't got any brakes!" He may have said more.

The broken skid chain had slapped against the hydraulic brake hose and destroyed the braking system.

The truck gained speed, gas cans clattering, faster and faster down the hill. They roared through the crossroad, missing the horses, wagon and panicked farmer by inches.

"Soupy was swerving right and left, trying to keep control as the runaway truck coasted to a stop." With no brakes, they continued on.

They unloaded the gas cans and repaired the brakes. They had been working for twenty hours.

The Second Lieutenant at the gas dump yelled to them, "Don't load! Turn the truck around and GET OUT!" The Germans were fast overtaking the area. Soupy gunned the truck and spun it around.

"We hadn't driven more than a few hundred yards when we heard the first explosion." The Second Lieutenant had thrown a hand grenade into the stockpile of gas cans.

A chain reaction began ((BOOM, BOOM, B-O-O-M)) with flames hundreds of feet high.

Al was sure the Second Lieutenant must have died in the fire to keep the Germans from getting the fuel.

Now it was Christmas 1944. Many thousands of American GIs were completely surrounded.

Al learned the Germans were not taking any prisoners. They would line up captured men in a field and machine gun them.

The cloud cover was so low the American Air Corps could not come to their rescue. Al and his outfit spent Christmas Day in a damp, penetrating cold.

By December 28, 1944, they all felt frozen. Al said, "There was fresh snow with no shelter, no fires, and no place to warm up or get dry." Many GIs suffered from frost bite and cold exposure.

Advance

Finally the weather began to clear and the sun came out. That meant air cover. As soon as the clouds lifted, whole squadrons of fighter planes started coming over.

Al said, "Those fighter pilots had guts. They would drop the bombs, strafe the German lines until their ammunition was gone, then come down for a dry run to scare the Germans."

The air cover from the fighter pilots finally broke the Germans' ring around the GIs. And the Germans didn't get the gas, thanks to Al, Soupy and the others who moved as much gas as they could.

Al said, "And thanks to the Second Lieutenant who blew up the rest of the gas and himself to keep the Germans from getting it."

The GIs captured a big German Panzer Division that had run out of fuel. Now the Allied advance was too fast and too immense for artillery operations.

The Americans met only scattered pockets of disorganized, surrendering Germans.

Al said, "The Americans stopped capturing prisoners because prisoners had to be fed." So German soldiers were disarmed and left behind.

Now it was February 1945. American troops came to the Remagen Bridge over the Rhine. The Germans had wired the bridge with dynamite, but the Americans got there before the Germans could blow it up.

It was a major turning point when the GIs began to cross

the Remagen Bridge back into Germany. As far as Al and his artillery outfit were concerned, it was just a matter of time until the war was over.

Frankenburg

In March 1945 Al's outfit was ordered to Frankenburg, a German village of women, children and old men. The First Sergeant told the villagers they had one hour get out before the GIs moved in. Al would now have shelter for the first time in many months.

Al and his army buddies Keenley and Little Joe stayed on the second floor of a house with no water and no electricity. They learned that the house belonged to two women, Frau Schmidt and her daughter.

Keenley knew a few German words. He also knew the non-fraternizing law with a sixty dollar fine if a GI was caught talking to any civilian.

Frau Schmidt pleaded with the GIs to not destroy her house. She offered to wash the GIs' clothes. Frau Schmidt's daughter was a war widow with a baby boy. The GIs saw that the baby was undernourished.

Al was able to sneak into the outfit's kitchen tent and steal powdered milk for the Schmidt women's baby, and also cocoa and chocolate bars for the women.

The grateful women gave Al and Keenley a baby bottle with a little schnapps in it.

The GIs stayed in Frankenburg for about six weeks. Al had very little to do except for guard duty. German prisoners of war did the outfit's KP duty.

Then Hitler committed suicide. The entire battalion in one huge convoy packed up and moved to Nancy, France.

Nancy because the European war was transferred Al to an Ordnance outfit. olice, a snappy job."

it army camp barber. He made three ig fifteen cents a haircut. All the GIs go home.

Al boarded a train with other GIs home. They rode in small French plank floor for the two-day trip.

ort camp that was filled with six-

was served thick ham slices with les. But after three years of combat a tiny stomach and could only eat a

Le Havre, France. The GIs marched docks and then onto a small tub of

lank to the main deck and down teel floor of the hold."

ing home. They slept on the steel 1. They ate meager meals on long ery hungry all the time.

egg and cornflakes. Lunch was wich and an apple. Supper was a r time at sea took fifteen days.

ig GIs got off the ship in Boston by an army band and Red Cross nurses.

The GIs were marched into an auditorium where [...] congratulated them for coming back alive. The office[...] them for their service.

The GIs were served dinner in a huge mess hall. All t[...] were German prisoners of war. Al said, "They served [...] a huge tender steak on a platter and a quart of fresh [...]

Al could only eat a little because his stomach was [...] from the meager ship fare and the many months of [...] rations. Al weighed 118 pounds.

The Boston train station was packed with GIs head[...] All along the train route Al saw huge "Welcome Back"[...] people waving at the returning troops.

At his final military base Al received his discharge [...] eighteen dollars for travel money. "I was out the door[...] ink was dry."

Al took the 5:30 train to Chicago. About a hundre[...] on the train bound for home. Al found a place to tel[...] wife Stella. He told her he was discharged, he was a c[...] he was coming home.

Al rode a streetcar and then walked the three block[...] his wife Stella lived with her parents. Then came a lo[...] reunion with Stella and Alex Junior, now four years [...]

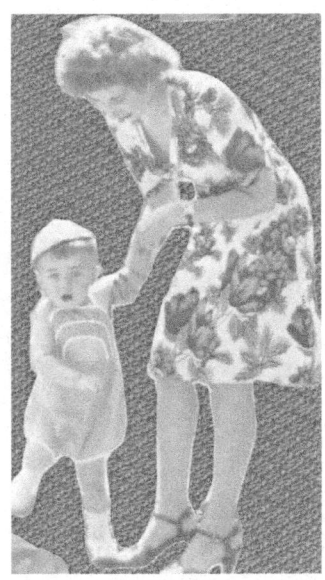

Stella Labak with Alex Junior in Chicago in 1944

Christmas 1944

The cauldron of World War II was a lived reality for some of my older generation of family members. December 1944 was a pivotal time for soldiers from the Kingsley family and from my husband Alex's Labak family.

In 1944 Cousin Adam Klosowski was starving in a German prisoner of war camp.

Infantry soldiers run for cover, WWII military photo archive

My great uncle, Lieutenant Colonel Wallace Kingsley, was an Army Air Corps officer helping plot a defense against German panzer divisions.

Alex's father Al Labak Sr froze his feet on guard duty when his artillery was surrounded by Germans.

Alex's uncle Bruno Zawislak fought in General Patton's infantry as they rescued Al Sr's artillery at the Battle of the Bulge. The Allies prevailed and the German Army collapsed.

A Parisian Woman

In the 1990s my Denver friend Suzanne Rabaud told me about her teenage years in Nazi-occupied France.

Suzanne Rabaud lived in Paris. Her father was an opera singer at the Paris Opera House. From Suzanne's apartment window she saw people shot dead on the street by German police.

Suzanne Rabaud's parents heard rumors that Suzanne's boyfriend was a Nazi sympathizer, so her parents forbade their courtship.

After the war Suzanne learned the true story. The rumors were a cover for her boyfriend's actual work for the French Resistance.

Suzanne told me a story of pre-war Paris when she spent carefree weekends exploring the Louvre Art Museum with her friends.

In a deserted basement gallery of antiquities, the giggling girls applied bright red lipstick to an Egyptian mummy.

In 1944 when Al Sr and his pals took a jeep ride into Paris, he might have seen Suzanne among the cheering crowds lining the boulevards.

CHAPTER 9   CHICAGOLAND

Krakow To South Side

I married Alex Labak in 1967. My beloved mother-in-law Stella told me stories of her Labak and Zawislak families. Al Senior's parents were immigrants from Poland who settled in Chicago's south side.

Stanislaw Labak 1889 - 1946 was from a farm near Krakow, Poland. Stanislaw's mother became a widow when her husband died of suicide.

When she remarried, the new step-father made Stanislaw's life so miserable that he left home at age fourteen.

Stanislaw made his way to America and then to Chicago. Stanislaw worked as a construction laborer, walking up inclined planks carrying loads of mortar on his shoulders.

The work was back-breaking and dangerous. Stanislaw helped build the first skyscrapers that changed the Chicago skyline.

Al Senior's mother was Anna Kuras Labak 1889 - 1969. Anna's family lived near Krakow, Poland where they made smoked sausages and hams from pigs they raised.

One time a fire broke out on Anna's farm. As a young girl Anna led the frightened horses away from the burning barn.

Anna was fourteen when she traveled to America. On the crowded immigrant ship Anna was forced to hide from ship workers who would bother her.

In Chicago Anna found work and married Stanislaw in 1907. They raised Al Senior and four daughters.

Frank Zawislak 1889 - 1971 was Stella Labak's father. Frank grew up in a village near Krakow, Poland. In 1910 when Frank was 21 years old Poland was invaded and partitioned by Germany, Russia and Austria.

Young men like Frank were ordered to serve in non-Polish militias. Frank escaped the draft and made his way to America and Chicago. Frank married Mary Skopek in 1917.

Frank loved to tell his children stories about his childhood. In his native Polish language Frank would describe all the village horses in colorful detail.

Frank worked in a Chicago steel mill for International Harvester. His job was to carry a long-handled ladle filled with white hot metal, then pour the metal into a mold. Flying sparks burned his clothes.

Every morning at breakfast Frank poured bacon fat into his coffee. He believed the hot drink protected his lungs from the toxic fumes of the steel mill.

Immigrant laborers like Frank were paid by the piece. Any imperfections meant no pay. Frequent layoffs during the Great Depression meant no pay. Frank was a strong advocate for labor unions. Silicosis slowly took his lung function and then his life.

Stella Labak's mother was Mary Skopek Zawislak 1889-1960. Mary came to Chicago from Poland in 1910.

Stella said her mother Mary had been an attractive, fashionable young woman who had an aristocratic look about her. As an immigrant, Mary's first job in Chicago was mopping hotel floors sixty hours a week.

Mary married Frank Zawislak in 1917 and they raised four children. At age 55 Mary suffered a stroke that left her bedridden and unable to speak. Mary's husband Frank and their adult children provided all of Mary's bedside care.

Second Generation

Bruno Zawislak 1919 - 1978 was Stella's brother. Bruno was a veteran of World War II. He served in the infantry in four major European campaigns.

After victory in Europe, or V-E Day, Bruno's infantry unit received a new order. Prepare for a ground invasion of Japan. But Japan surrendered after atomic bombs leveled Hiroshima and Nagasaki.

Bruno Zawislak was a deeply religious Catholic. He wore a business suit and a fedora traveling the Chicago elevated train to his downtown job as a land purchaser for the State of Illinois. Bruno was a stock market investor and he enjoyed reading the Wall Street Journal.

Florence Zawislak and her brother Bruno J Zawislak
about 1950 in Chicago

Florence Zawislak 1926 – 2001 was Stella Labak's sister. For forty years Florka worked at Sears Roebuck headquarters in

Chicago.

Her downtown Chicago attire was fashionable suits and alligator pumps. Florka owned her own home in the suburb of Westchester and she invested in the stock market.

Stella's sister Emily Zawislak 1923 - 2006 was a teacher in Chicago Public Schools. Emily loved to travel, visiting Machu Picchu, the Canada Rockies and Nome, Alaska.

Stella's three siblings Bruno, Florence and Emily never married, but they helped their sister Stella and Stella's children in many ways.

Al Labak Sr 1919 - 1990 was my husband Alex's father. Al Sr was a U.S. Army veteran. Another chapter of this book describes his years of World War II combat.

Al Sr disliked army discipline. He hated his first sergeant, who never promoted Al Sr beyond private first class.

After the war Al Sr was a dutiful husband and provider for his wife Stella. He was a skilled mechanic at Chicago's massive Nabisco Bakery.

He was a lifelong labor union member. Al Sr and Stella raised five children: Alex, Judy, Steve, Robert and Lori.

Al Sr tolerated his crowded household of children. He took summer fishing trips to Minnesota, leaving Stella and the children behind in the sweltering city.

The Labak family of seven lived in a small brick bungalow in south Chicago. Al Sr liked to escape to his basement chair with his cigars and bottles of beer.

Alex's mother Stella Zawislak Labak 1921 - 2014 loved her five children, her two daily newspapers, and Chicago's vibrant culture. She baked a quarter million chocolate chip cookies. Stella's two sisters and brother were her life support.

Stella Zawiskak and Al Labak 1942 in Chicago

Stella's husband Al Sr was a difficult man to live with. Late in her life, Stella revealed to her son Alex that, very soon after her marriage, Stella realized she had made a terrible mistake.

But she could never divorce. The Catholic Church forbade it. Polish tradition forbade it. America in the nineteen-forties forbade it. And Stella, age twenty in 1942, was already pregnant with Alex Junior.

CHAPTER 10   LANDING PLACE

Immigrants

Here we will stop a moment and step off our trampoline of space and time. Stand once more on safe, solid ground. Ancestor stories are inspiring and heartwarming, yet terrifying and tragic in equal measure.

As we look back through the stories, we might want to ask a question. Why did some ancestors risk everything, pull up stakes and start over somewhere new?

History tells us that we humans have migrated from homelands to new lands for 300,000 years. Why do people move on to another town or another state or another continent?

Our European ancestors with names like Kingsley, Murray, Labak, Zawislak, joined the great migrations that crossed the ocean to the New World.

For some of our ancestors, leaving the family home came early. Anna Labak left Poland at age fourteen. Frank Zawislak escaped his abusive step-father at age fourteen. Edward E Kingsley left Wisconsin when he was sixteen.

Hunger

Some ancestors left their homeland because of a venturing spirit and unbounded curiosity. But for many ancestors, poverty and an empty stomach were a good enough reason.

When Alex's grandfather Stanislaw left Poland, he first traveled to Hungary. But conditions there were so bad that dogs were killed and eaten for food. So Stanislaw made his way to America.

During the Great Depression of the 1930s, it took another generation for Chicago's immigrant families to climb their way out of poverty and hunger.

Alex's Uncle Bruno Zawislak said as a child he would sneak a drink of milk from the family ice box, then pour water into the milk bottle and hope his sisters wouldn't notice.

Poverty

American farmers endured a different type of poverty well into the 1950s. Many farm families lived without the basic services that town and city cousins took for granted. My mother Helen Hawkes Murray raised small children, one was me, with no electricity.

Then in 1950 we moved to a farmhouse with electrical wiring but no water. We used outhouse and chamber pot until 1954 when we moved to a new farm house with indoor toilet, bathtub, and a real kitchen sink.

Resourceful farmers like my father Roy Murray learned how to repair their own machinery. A farmer could build from scratch a chicken coop or cowshed, oil shed or outhouse.

Every few years our Murray farm income dried up because of crop failure or a collapse of crop prices. Then our family of seven lived on milk money and farm loans.

Poverty was a way of life for my husband Alex's Chicago family in the 1930s. Immigrants from Eastern Europe lived in cold water flats with one large Catholic family per floor in three-story brick houses.

In every Polish kitchen, cloth diapers hung overhead like banners to dry. A grandmother said, "Royalty in residence." During the Great Depression job layoffs meant no wages for weeks at a time.

Old Ways

East European immigrants brought their language, religious beliefs and folk traditions to the New World. The women of my new Polish family in 1967 wanted me to wear an embroidered white apron as part of my wedding day. Years later I discovered why.

Traditional European folk dress features white embroidered aprons. For thousands of years across prehistoric Europe, small carved female figurines represented fertility beliefs.

A white apron symbolized a young woman's fervent hope for a kind husband and survivable childbirth.

After the Christian Era, prayers to the Virgin Mary and the symbolic white apron continued for East European immigrants. Right up to my marriage into Polish family tradition in 1967.

An immigrant's native language can fade in a generation. My own great grandmother Christina Anderson Kingsley was born in Sweden and came to America at age 17. Did she share Swedish stories and songs with her ten children?

My husband Alex's grandparents in Chicago spoke Polish at home, at work, at the grocery, the butcher shop, and at their Polish Catholic parish.

Even the family doctor spoke Polish. They read a Polish newspaper. The children did not learn English until they started public school.

I was warmly welcomed into my husband Alex's extended family in the 1960s. We all gathered around the piano to sing traditional Polish Christmas carols. Alex's Aunt Florence said the Polish carols had deep cultural meaning and could not easily be translated into harsh English words.

Finding Our Way

All of us come from complicated family histories. We all have moments of joy, love, fear. Anger, grief, exhaustion, happiness. Some of us hold on to lifelong secrets, judgments, false stories.

Some families share loving, devoted, mostly joyful bonds. And some families endure a lifetime of unhappy entrapment. Some of us are misfits and rebels. Some of us struggle with failing health, mental illness, past trauma, addiction, crime, financial ruin.

A chance discovery can shake your life to the core. You might be told your Ma and Pa are not your real parents. You might discover your name doesn't match your birth certificate name.

Families can separate and disconnect with estrangements, divorce, babies given up. Step-parents, step-siblings, step-cousins, step-grandchildren can join a family but later get lost in the shuffle.

Children sometimes grow up with no siblings, or with no cousins, aunts, uncles, or grandparents. Their friends become their family.

Relationships can be confusing. A widow and her daughter might marry a widower and his son. One older relative explained to me how it happened that he became his own uncle.

One woman relative became happily married to the widower of her aunt. We can sort it out. Enduring love stories are not all that complicated.

Kinship, family, and cultural background can be stronger than a biological DNA connection. The most carefully recorded family history cannot guarantee the genetic connection of a passed-down paternal name like Murray or Kingsley or Labak.

Family histories can describe cultural bonds but not provable DNA connections. We overlook one particular power women have held through the generations. A paternal DNA line might be severed when a wife secretly strays from the marital bed.

DNA tests can reveal startling news about a person's lineage and ethnicity. Let's face it. Our DNA connection to a proud ancestral name might have disconnected long ago.

Family ties over many generations include children welcomed into the family by many means. This happy and fortunate blending of new blood lines and new connections can strengthen and enrich all of us.

Your Story Here

Family history is a tightly wrapped package that we open one layer at a time. Ancestor stories of struggle, sacrifice and survival help us understand our own place in the world. We discover that the life decisions of our ancestors can affect the trajectory of our own lives.

Any recorded family history, like this book in your hand, skids to a stop on the year of publication.

My own lifetime, starting 1947, spanned the industrial age, nuclear age, space age. Then on past computers, internet, and AI to the quantum age.

Our descendants will live in new societies with their own migration stories. Our grandchildren will write the next chapter of human connection. How they got on, how they persevered, how they made their best life.

Grand Tetons, Wyoming, from family photos

Sources

These ancestor stories were discovered in books, family genealogies, newspapers, newsletters, recordings, websites, and notes from oral interviews.

I am grateful to Ronald Kingsley and Danny Hawkes for sharing their family histories with me.

All errors and omissions are solely my own.

A sampling of sources is listed below.

Mayflower; voyage, community, war. Nathaniel Philbrick. 2006.

The 1619 project; a new origin story. Nikole Hannah-Jones and the New York Times Magazine. 2019.

These truths; a history of the United States. Jill Lepore. 2018.

Kannah Creek. Carol Anderson. 2005.

Red hole in time. 1988. Island in the sky. 1999. Western Colorado histories by Muriel Marshall.

Kingsley family of America. William Arthur Kingsley. 1980.

Edward E. and Christina Kingsley family history. Ronald A. Kingsley. 2009.

Askov American, a newspaper of Pine County, Minnesota. Three interviews with Adam Klosowski, World War II veteran. 1995.

Wheatland Eagle, a newspaper of Wheatland, North Dakota. 1904 and 1905.

Western Christian Advocate, a newspaper of the Methodist Episcopal Church. Editorials by Bishop Calvin Kingsley. 1856 to 1864.

Uncompahgre Journal, a newsletter of Chipeta Chapter. The Colorado Archaeological Society. Articles and photos from 2003 to 2015 by Laurie Labak.

The Hawkes family news, a newsletter by Marjorie Lancaster. Farmington, Connecticut. 2002.

Family history and genealogy. Mary J. Dunstan. Burbank, California. 1982.

Our Polish heritage. A family history by Laurie Labak. 1982.

Family history on audiotape and CD compiled by Danny Hawkes. Klamath Falls, Oregon. 2004.

Stella Zawislak Labak. Oral family history of Poland and Chicago. Interviews and notes with Laurie Labak, 1980.

Al Labak, Senior. Oral history of World War II campaigns across Europe. Interviews and notes with Laurie Labak. 1980.

Websites consulted in 2025. Familysearch.org. Wikitree.com. Genealogy.com. Ancestry.com.

Made in the USA
Coppell, TX
25 February 2026

72383048R00066